VOICES *of* RECOVERY

The articles in this text were reprinted with permission from the *Psychiatric Rehabilitation Journal*. Citations for the original publications are included as footnotes at the bottom of the first page of each article.

Published by:
Center for Psychiatric Rehabilitation
College of Health and Rehabilitation Sciences (Sargent College)
Boston University
940 Commonwealth Avenue West
Boston, MA 02215
www.bu.edu/cpr/

The Center for Psychiatric Rehabilitation is partially funded by the National Institute on Disability and Rehabilitation Research and the Center for Mental Health Services, Substance Abuse and Mental Health Services Administration.

Printed in the United States of America

Library of Congress Control Number: 2009922413
ISBN13: 978-1-878512-23-9

Published 2009

VOICES *of* RECOVERY

Edited by Sue McNamara

Boston University Center for Psychiatric Rehabilitation

CONTENTS

PREFACE

In 1994, the Center for Psychiatric Rehabilitation at Boston University published *The Experience of Recovery,* edited by LeRoy Spaniol and Martin Koehler. It is an anthology of stories and poems by people recounting their own recovery experiences. The book was published at a time when the notion of recovery in the mental health field was a relatively new concept. *The Experience of Recovery* has been read by consumers, family members, practitioners, trainers, administrators, and members of boards of directors. It is a book that anyone connected to the mental health field would enjoy reading. It has been used in academic classes and has been left on coffee tables in residential settings and mental health programs for anyone to pick up and read. The first-person accounts are inspirational, and they have helped many people to feel hopeful for their own future and to make progress in their own recovery journey. Customers who have purchased *The Experience of Recovery* began asking when another book of its kind would be published by our Center.

As a result, *Voices of Recovery* was created as an updated and expanded version of *The Experience of Recovery. Voices of Recovery* consists of two different types of "voices" in the mental health field. The first "voice" is a collection of personal accounts that were published in the "Coping With" column of the *Psychiatric Rehabilitation Journal* from the years 2000 through 2008. Since the 1990s, the "Coping With" column was included in each issue of the journal to provide an opportunity for publishing personal accounts of individuals' experiences of recovery. As more and more people write their unique personal stories, this venue for publication allows these articles to be widely read and shared with others publically in a professional journal. Equally inspiring, these articles describe individuals' experiences of coping with mental illness and of leading them to their own personal recovery.

The second "voice" is a collection of Photovoice projects that were part of the Recovery Center classes held at the Center for Psychiatric Rehabilitation. The photovoice concept was developed by Professor Caroline Wang, at the University of Michigan School of Public Health, and Mary Ann Burris, from the Ford Foundation. Photovoice is a process that has been used for research, education, social change, and the development of more healthful public policy. Cameras were provided to individuals with serious mental illnesses, and they used photovoice to amplify their visions and experience. Short stories or messages were written to explain the person meaning behind the image from the photographer's point of view. By uniting the immediate impact of a photograph and the story, it contextualizes and enhances it. Through the power of the visual image, photovoice offers an innovative way to break the silence that often surrounds the experience of mental illness. Photovoice has three main goals:

- To enable people to record and reflect their community's strengths and concerns.

- To promote critical dialogue and knowledge about personal and community issues through large and small group discussions of photographs.

- To reach policy makers.

To these ends, the photovoice process lays out multiple stages for defining the goals of a project, anticipating an audience, taking pictures and telling stories about them, evaluation, and presentation. While photovoice can be done on a more individual basis, one of the most powerful aspects of the technique is the group reflection on and discussion of the photographs. The storytelling aspect of photovoice follows the acronym *SHOWED*:

- What do you *See* here?

- What's really *Happening* here?

- How does this relate to *Our* lives?

- *Why* does this problem/condition/strength exist?

- How could this image *Educate* the community, policy makers, etc.?

- What can we *Do* about it (the problem, condition, or strength)?

By stimulating critical dialogue of the issues raised in the photographs, photovoice participants generate awareness, not just of problems or concerns, but also of potential solutions and areas of strength with respect to their lives and communities. The images and stories can be shared with an audience in numerous ways including: presentations, exhibits, books, videos, CD-ROM, and on the Internet. Two advances in photography, disposable and digital cameras, offer inexpensive ways of generating images and a wide range of formats for presenting those images. Thus, photovoice can be carried out in almost any setting with almost any group of people.

Voices of Recovery was created with the purpose to be read on its own or to accompany the *Recovery Workbook: Practical Coping and Empowerment Strategies for People with Psychiatric Disability* (1994) written by LeRoy Spaniol, Martin Koehler, and Dori Hutchinson. *The Recovery Workbook* is used by individuals or in groups to help people understand and navigate their own recovery process. The articles and the photovoice projects in *Voices of Recovery* have been organized to supplement the

chapters of *The Recovery Workbook*. These chapters include:

- Recovery, which outlines the phases and aspects of the recovery process.

- Increasing Knowledge and Control, which discusses the impact of serious mental illness and the services and values of a recovery-oriented mental health system.

- Managing Life's Stresses, which talks about the symptoms and sources of stress as well as coping strategies.

- Enhancing Personal Meaning, which promotes the idea of acknowledging our accomplishments and personal enrichment.

- Building Personal Support, which discusses connecting with others, basic communication skills, asking for support, and setting boundaries on our relationships.

- Setting Personal Goals, which outlines a step-by-step guide for setting personal goals and developing a plan for achieving a personal goal.

When reading *Voices of Recovery,* we believe that the personal accounts and the photovoice projects will inspire hope and optimism for recovery for individuals with psychiatric disabilities, their family members, and mental health professionals. In addition, given the heartfelt nature of the articles and photovoice projects, we believe that this book will appeal to anyone in the general community and could be used as an educational tool to help reduce stigma and stereotypes of mental illness.

We would like to acknowledge and thank all of the people who contributed their articles and photovoice projects to this book. We appreciate their bravery and strength they have shown through their lived experiences, their willingness to share their stories, as well as their hopes and inspiration to others. When we asked permission to have their articles and photovoice projects published in this book, most people said that they felt honored to have their experiences shared and felt hopeful that their messages might be helpful to someone else. We appreciate this type of caring, giving, and community spirit.

We also would like to acknowledge and thank Bill Anthony for his recovery vision, his leadership in the mental health field and at our Center, and for his encouragement to develop this book; LeRoy Spaniol for his inspiration in developing our first recovery products and for founding both the *Psychiatric Rehabilitation Journal* and the "Coping With" column in the journal; Kathy Furlong-Norman for her support of this project as the current managing editor of the *Psychiatric Rehabilitation Journal;* Dori Hutchinson for her guidance with this project as director of our services division; Alexandra (Sasha) Bowers for introducing us to photovoice; Derek Fuller for his work in facilitating photovoice classes at our Recovery Center and for his assistance in providing photovoice projects for this book; Andrea Bengston and Jake Briggs for their assistance in gathering contact information for the photovoice authors; and Linda Getgen for her endless support and for her creativity in designing and publishing this book.

Sue McNamara
Center for Psychiatric Rehabilitation

References and Resources

Anthony, W. A. (2007). *Toward a vision of recovery form mental health and psychiatric rehabilitation services, 2nd edition.* Boston: Center for Psychiatric Rehabilitation, Boston University.

Booth, T. & Booth W. (2003). In the frame: Photovoice and mothers with learning difficulties. *Disability & Society,* 18(4): 431–442.

Davidson, L., Harding, C., & Spaniol, L. (Eds). 2005. *Recovery from severe mental illnesses: Research evidence and implications for practice. Volume 1.* Boston: Center for Psychiatric Rehabilitation, Boston University.

Davidson, L., Harding, C., & Spaniol, L. (Eds). 2006. *Recovery from severe mental illnesses: Research evidence and implications for practice. Volume 2.* Boston: Center for Psychiatric Rehabilitation, Boston University.

Harrison, B. (2002). Photographic visions and narrative inquiry. *Narrative Inquiry.* 12(1): 87–111.

http://www.bu.edu/cpr/photovoice/index.html

Johnson, D., Russinova, Z., & Gagne, C. (2009). Using Photovoice to fight the stigma of mental illness. *Recovery & Rehabilitation Newsletter,* 4(4). Boston: Center for Psychiatric Rehabilitation, Boston University.

Killion, C. M. & Wang, C. C. (2000). Linking African American mothers across life stage and station through photovoice. *Journal of Health Care for the Poor & Underserved.* 11(3):310–25.

LeClerc, C. M., Wells, D. L., Craig, D., & Wilson J. L . (2002). Falling short of the mark: Tales of life after hospital discharge. *Clinical Nursing Research.* 11(3):242–263; discussion 264–266.

Lykes, M. B., Blanche, M. T., & Hamber, B. (2003). Narrating survival and change in Guatemala and South Africa: The politics of representation and a liberatory community psychology. *American Journal of Community Psychology.* 31(1–2):79–90.

Mertle, A. (Producer). (2007). *Beyond the shadow of stigma* [video presentation]. Cambridge, MA: Cambridge Community Television, Crazyant Films. Retrieved February 10, 2009 from http://www.cctvcambridge.org/node/1695

Spaniol, L., Bellingham, R., Cohen, B., & Spaniol, S. (2003). *The recovery workbook II: Connectedness.* Boston: Center for Psychiatric Rehabilitation, Boston University.

Spaniol, L., & Koehler, M. (1994). *Experience of recovery.* Boston: Center for Psychiatric Rehabilitation, Boston University.

Spaniol, L., Koehler, M., & Hutchinson, D. (1994). *The recovery workbook Practical coping and empowerment strategies for people with psychiatric disability.* Boston: Center for Psychiatric Rehabilitation, Boston University.

Spaniol, L., & Spaniol, S. (2003). *The recovery workbook II: Connectedness: Leader's guide.* Boston: Center for Psychiatric Rehabilitation, Boston University.

Wang, C. C. (1998). Project: Photovoice involving homeless men and women of Washtenaw County, Michigan. *Health Education and Behavior,* 25 (1): 9–10.

Wang, C. C. (1999). Photovoice: A participatory action research strategy applied to women's health. *Journal of Women's Health,* 8(2):185–92.

Wang, C. C. Using photovoice as a participatory assessment and issue selection tool: A case study with the homeless in Ann Arbor. (2003). In M. Minkler & N. Wallerstein (Eds.), *Community based participatory research for health.* San Francisco: Jossey-Bass.

Wang, C. & Burris, M. A. (1994). Empowerment through photovoice: Portraits of participation. *Health Education Quarterly,* 21(2): 171–186.

Wang, C. & Burris, M. A. (1997). Photovoice: Concept, methodology, and use for participatory needs assessment. *Health Education & Behavior,* 24(3):369–87.

Wang, C., Burris, M. A., & Xiang, Y. P. (1996). Chinese village women as visual anthropologists: A participatory approach to reaching policymakers. *Social Science and Medicine,* 42(10): 1391– 1400.

Wang, C.C., Cash, J. L., & Powers, L. S. (2000). Who knows the streets as well as the homeless?: Promoting personal and community action through photovoice. *Health Promotion Practice,* 1(1): 81–89.

Wang, C. C. & Redwood-Jones, Y. A. (2001). Photovoice ethics: Perspectives from Flint Photovoice. *Health Education & Behavior,* 28(5): 560–72.

Wang, C. C., Yi, W. K., & Tao, Z. W. (1998). Photovoice as a participatory health promotion strategy. *Health Promotion International,* 13(1): 75–86.

Wang, C., Yuan, Y. L., & Feng, M. L. (1996). Photovoice as a tool for participatory evaluation: The community's view of process and impact. *Journal of Contemporary Health,* 4: 47–49.

CHAPTER I

Recovery

From Psychosis and Alienation to Recovery

Christine Mahoney Holst

Two weeks after giving birth I wanted to know why my baby winced and her face turned purple for no apparent reason. I noticed that I could cause the effect when I gently circled her inside ankle knuckle. According to my baby's hospital records, she exhibited the same symptoms shortly after birth. I called the Neo-Natal Intensive Care Unit of El Camino Hospital in Mountain View, California, where my baby spent the first week of her life. A nurse on duty spooked me by telling me how serious my baby's condition could become.

Two days later on May 21, 1994, forces assembled and trapped me into an involuntary psychiatric commitment. The diagnosis was post-partum psychosis. I was 2 weeks and 2 days post-partum with my first and only child, when my husband, mother-in-law, newborn, and I entered the El Camino Hospital Emergency Room. My husband and his mother took turns speaking privately with hospital staff members. I did not have a clue as to why we were there. We were supposed to be going to an appointment at the pediatrician's office in Los Altos, California.

Recipe for a Breakdown

As I sat in the emergency room waiting area, I grew tired, weak, and exhausted. When I could not remain awake any longer, I succinctly told my husband, "I need sleep." He motioned to a place out of the way on the carpeted floor where I could lie down, using my soft, leather covered credenza to rest my head.

I eagerly slipped down and fell asleep. Seconds later, hospital staff members startled me awake. Next they escorted me to a room, sat me in a chair, and abandoned me, which made me feel insignificant. I said a little prayer to God, "I give up." Then I immediately broke down.

Seated in the chair, my eyes went into Rapid Eye Movement (REM). Then tremors surged through my muscles giving me what felt like a full body massage. My head rolled gently from side to side. My shoulders heaved up and down. My chest dropped forward to my knees and my arms to my fingertips stretched out and released. This convulsing continued for what seemed like half an hour.

Alienating Accusations

This full-blown breakdown was never mentioned again. Instead, I was locked into a 72-hour hold, classified as gravely disabled, citing that I was over-stimulating my baby with massages. I was told that I was a danger to my baby, a claim based on statistics, so said the psychiatrist. They criticized my judgement and thoughts, telling me I was delusional, out of touch with reality, and in denial. I was blind-sided by these accusations since I was unfamiliar with my surroundings and my situation. Furthermore, my mom was not notified of my crisis prior to hospitalization, and my mother-in-law denied that anything was wrong with me. These two insults breached fiduciary responsibility, and impaired my ability to reason.

This article was published in the *Psychiatric Rehabilitation Journal*, 2000, 23(4), 397–400, and is reprinted with permission.

Other reasons for impairment to my thinking were the psychiatrist's unwillingness to develop trust as well as her plan to overmedicate me. A nurse refused to administer the prescribed Haldol when I requested it. There was no follow-up therapy or explanation for being secluded, punished, restrained, and forcibly med-icated by injection.

> I knew that I needed help, but I wanted it without being locked up, punished, threatened, or mistrusted.

and forcibly med-icated by injection. There were no priv-ileges during con-finement to get sec-ond opinions from my primary mental health providers. The psychiatrist withdrew the writ of habeas corpus and released me from the hospital when my insurance ran out. I could not help but speculate that I was hos-pitalized to keep the psychiatric unit functioning, and not because I was sick.

During my hospitalizations I did not want to return home. My husband was suffering from an anx-iety disorder. He was put under a doctor's care a cou-ple of days before our baby was born. I felt inappro-priately targeted as a source of his anxieties. I could not express the joy I felt about our baby without con-flict arising between my husband and me. I felt my husband was jealous over the bond I felt and expressed about our daughter. His criticism of my joy caused me to feel mentally unsafe with him. Return-ing home was not a desirable option because my hus-band declared in a letter his intention to file for divorce.

For the following three years, I was in and out of more than 12 different hospitals, in 4 states, resulting in more than 10 involuntary commitments and a vari-ety of diagnoses. I was running scared from the entrapments of the psychiatric system. Somehow I knew that I needed help, but I wanted it without being locked up, punished, threatened, or mistrusted. I needed the legal intervention of a Superior Court judge to either free me from future psychiatric com-mitments or commit me to treatment until I was well.

Distorted Reality

I believed I was doing the right thing by refusing Haldol, an anti-psychotic medication, especially after my assigned nurse refused to administer it to me because she did not see any symptoms requiring it. The incident undermined my thinking and ability to trust. I turned inward, hoping and trusting that God had a plan for me. I prayed hard for God to give me a sign. Reality took on a whole new meaning as I became watchful, awaiting signs from God.

Following my release from El Camino Hospital, I believed that I was the promised Jesus Christ incar-nate. Being ever watchful, I heard in a song that my favorite uncle died; I sent condolences to my aunt. I was fearful that if I did not interpret the song as a sign, my uncle would be in grave danger. It seemed to me that my thinking could be as statistically sound as were the accusations that I would harm my daughter.

Fortunately my "information" about my uncle was wrong. And, for my peace of mind, my aunt and uncle have forgiven me for the upheaval caused by my letters. Further, my aunt and uncle have been good and generous to me, following my progress and recov-ery, and welcoming me back into their home in Cali-fornia when I travel there to visit my daughter.

Letter writing was my primary outlet for relieving frustration. After release from El Camino Hospital I took up writing letters to anyone, including Janet Reno, U.S. Attorney General, who I thought could help me get a writ of habeas corpus court hearing, but nothing came of it. Eventually, once I stopped lactat-ing (about 4 months post-partum), I headed for Penn-sylvania where I hoped to get help—for what I was not exactly sure. But my hope was for humane treat-ment.

Recovery in Pennsylvania

What finally set me on the road to recovery was getting my equivalent writ of habeas corpus hearings in Pennsylvania. Twice, a judge ordered a 6-month hospital commitment with treatment. I fought the first ruling with every bit of courage I could muster until I felt recognized as an individual, and not as a statistic.

The professional staff members at Haverford State Hospital rallied around me without punishment, restraints, injections of medication, or solitary confinement.

Presently, I am in full recovery, living in Downingtown, Pennsylvania, and working full time as a sales administrative assistant, a job I enjoy and need in order to afford my medications. Through a special county subsidy program, called CHIPPs, I live in a Community Rehabilitation Residence (CRR), which is a board and maximum care housing arrangement operated by Kelsch Associates. I adhere to goal-planning, bi-weekly psychotherapy sessions, monthly medication reviews, and weekly intensive case management meetings through Human Services, Inc.

I am grateful to the taxpayers, voters, and representatives of the county and state of Chester County, Pennsylvania, who made my recovery possible. Their support for the needs of mental health consumers both in and out of the hospital is tremendous. Twice, in my escapades between California and Pennsylvania, I had to return to my hometown in Pennsylvania to get better.

Partial Recovery

The first time back in Pennsylvania I was stabilized through the efforts of my brother, his wife, and my mom, as well as Crisis Residential, and Community Services for Human Growth. My brother and his wife gave me a place to stay. Mom linked me up with Crisis Residential. Crisis Residential offered a staffed house for me to stay in voluntarily for up to 14 days instead of a hospital. I needed Crisis Residential for relief from the side effects from the medications prescribed in Iowa. When I could no longer perform my duties at the butcher shop where I worked part-time through the influence of my brother, I retreated to Crisis Residential.

> I felt good about being treated as a whole person and not someone to be feared.

Upon release from Crisis Residential, I was placed in an outpatient program, called Partial, at Community Services for Human Growth, Inc. in Phoenixville, Pennsylvania. Partial was a place to go to during the week instead of staying at home. It helped restore my confidence and set goals that would help me move forward with my life. I resumed part-time work at the butcher shop. As I got stronger, I became able to work as a temporary administrative assistant. Community Services for Human Growth then placed me on outpatient psychotherapy one day per week and monthly medication reviews. Within 6 months I was able to return to California to be near my daughter.

I was stabilized, but not fully recovered, during my first stay in Pennsylvania. Full recovery would have meant that I could link symptoms with diagnosis and thereby justify psychotropic medication. With such knowledge, I could make good judgements regarding medications, report unusual behavior about myself, and obtain continuity in treatment while living anywhere in the USA.

Recipe for a Relapse

The risks of not understanding a diagnosis or symptoms became apparent after changing psychiatrists. In Pennsylvania, I was diagnosed as having bi-polar (manic-depressive) disorder, and in California, a change disorder. Because I was stable, I did not expect my California psychiatrist would change medications. However, after seeing me for several months, he decided on a change. I was forced to decide between him or the medications. I chose to trust my psychiatrist and accepted the medication change. He continued my lithium treatment but switched me from the anti-depressant, Wellbutrin, to Prozac.

I did not want to change medication because I felt I was functioning just fine, working and living in the community, and conforming to my treatment plan. However, because I had many months invested in my psychiatrist at the time, I did not want to terminate the relationship and start over elsewhere. I felt I needed his recommendation to see my daughter more often and without supervision. Not only that, but I saw a note in my legal brief at my divorce attorney's

4

office that another psychiatrist had recommended the same medication change. I could not reasonably turn down the Prozac since two psychiatrists concurred independently.

> It was very rewarding to see and meet consumers prospering in the community and contributing to progress in the mental health field at all levels.

The Prozac set off mania in me, which led to non-compliance with medications, a relapse of psychosis, periods of memory lapses, and a series of hospitalizations in California and Pennsylvania. I probably should add that I might have complicated matters by taking the herb gingko biloba while on Prozac.

Journey Toward Recovery

My California landlord intervened for my return to family in Pennsylvania for recovery. After 6 months of crazy behavior in Pennsylvania, splitting my time between acts of good faith and condemnations of others, I ended up being court-committed for up to 6 months of treatment in Haverford State Hospital.

It took me a couple of weeks to settle into my new environment at Haverford. I fought my stay by contacting the FBI, 911, and Patients Rights Advocates. I communicated by phone and by mail. Responses started to pour in. The superintendent of the hospital even got involved. He sat in on one of my treatment team sessions, which he followed up with a note to me, asking me to stop fighting the system and to pour my energies into working with my treatment team. That made a tremendously positive impression on me. First, someone cared enough to write a letter to me; second, the letter was from someone with authority; third, the letter was non-threatening; fourth, the letter contained some insight as to what was going on with my treatment team; and fifth, the letter expressed hope for my recovery.

Another thing that made a difference with me was my dad's involvement. Every week he sat in on my weekly treatment team meetings. Afterwards he would sit with me just to talk. During day-to-day conversation, he shared his favorable impressions of my caretakers. He helped me to come around and see things in a positive light. And one thing he did not do was to force the issue of medication, for which I was grateful.

At Haverford I was treated with the dignity one could expect with any illness; mine just happened to be a mental illness. I felt good about being treated as a whole person and not someone to be feared. The staff members explained the progression of moving from unit to unit until discharge, which provided me with hope. No one in any of my previous hospitalizations had taken the time to do that. Previous hospitalizations were paternalistic in nature and medication clouded any discussions of hope and recovery.

Privileges

A valuable bit of insight I finally learned at Haverford was that my psychiatrist was my team leader. As such, she approved any privileges, from grounds privileges, to day passes off campus, to work programs, to upgrading to a less structured treatment unit, to any activity that would take place beyond the doors of the locked unit. She seldom belabored the medication issue, except during scheduled treatment meetings. If I had a concern that required her attention in the meantime, such as privileges or medication, she would fit me into her schedule. Her presence on the unit nearly everyday made her approachable and helped me get on Zyprexa, an anti-psychotic medication with few side effects and that I will likely take for life.

My treatment team at Haverford reached out to find on-campus employment suitable to my skills and education. My outlook for the future brightened and soon more good things followed. I taught computer classes, wrote, and published two issues of the campus newsletter, and earned a scholarship to attend the Pennsylvania Mental Health Consumers' Association conference in Erie, Pennsylvania. It was very rewarding to see and meet consumers prospering in the community and contributing to progress in the mental health field at all levels.

One other service that contributed to my recovery is the Consumer Satisfaction Team (CST) of Chester County, Pennsylvania. CST checks in periodically with county mental health consumers to ensure all of their needs are being serviced appropriately and advocated as necessary. They visited me while I was hospitalized at Haverford and now while I am housed at a CRR. They advocate both good points and areas for improvement to my service providers. Little things have come up and have been promptly dealt with.

Gradually I am attaining my goals, of which I have many, including traveling to see my daughter in San Jose. I hope to see more of my daughter, without supervision, for overnight visits, and with privileges to transport her to outings when I am in town.

A firm
foundation and
growth everyday =
wellness.

Everyday I see this site. It reminds me of my wellness. At first a hole in the ground, then a structure
starts. Huge cranes putting things in place. A firm
foundation and growth everyday = wellness.
—Anonymous, from *Wellness As I See It,* 2003

Experience with Post-Secondary Education for Individuals with Severe Mental illness

Jennifer M. Padron

Higher education systems are not prepared to provide appropriate support for students with a psychiatric disability. "It's like saying to someone in a wheelchair, 'Go ahead and recover,' but you haven't installed ramps and curb cuts" (Rogers, 2004). States have laws to keep individuals with mental illness separated from the larger community. Thirty-seven states restrict the right of a person with mental illness to vote, 44 restrict the right to serve on a jury, 24 restrict the right to hold public office, 33 allow mental illness as grounds for divorce, and 27 use mental illness as grounds to terminate parental rights (Rogers, 2004). It's no wonder that individuals with psychiatric disabilities are not considered part of the community of higher education.

Requesting accommodations for a psychiatric disability is especially difficult because most colleges and universities toss psychiatric disability services into the broader category of general health services or physical disability programs, making it more difficult to navigate the system. Students with psychiatric disabilities are expected to take the initiative to research and apply for these services which are often difficult to locate. Publicly admitting to having a mental illness deters students from seeking services until an episode forces the need for accommodations at a time when the student is the least likely to be able to navigate the system independently.

> It is possible to…re-group, re-process goals and ambitions, and begin the process of living again.

Personal Loss

I've experienced a great deal of personal loss due to mental illness. Exacerbation of psychiatric symptoms caused me to lose a job that I loved. I fear that I won't be able to return to this work. My illness cost me a sense of self worth and personal identity. I became the illness, obsessed with the illness, and had difficulty interacting with others because of my preoccupation with the illness. The diagnosis of severe mental illness accompanied by the symptoms that brought on that diagnosis is like death. It's the death of the person you once were; family and friends also experience a sense of death. It takes years to work through the grieving process and reach a point where recovery is possible. Once this point is reached, it is possible to accept the limitations imposed by the illness, re-group, re-process goals and ambitions, and begin the process of living again.

A variety of medical professionals advised me to drop out of school and find a minimum wage job to eliminate stress. These professionals created a sense of doom and increased feelings of worthlessness for me. I felt like I would never be able to engage in challenging activities, never complete school and never work in a professional position again. Indifferent and judg-

This article was published in the *Psychiatric Rehabilitation Journal*, 2006, 30(2), 147–149, and is reprinted with permission.

mental professionals cause huge barriers to recovery. The professionals who believed that dropping out of school would reduce my stress did not understand my need for involvement in activities that promoted recovery. I actually completed the request to withdraw from the university, for medical reasons, convinced that I was worthless. It's easy to believe the negative when you are having a psychiatric crisis. Other members of the treatment team stepped up, encouraging me to remain in school and attempt to complete the semester. I stopped the withdrawal and took the risk. I successfully completed two out of three of my classes.

> Professionals who believed that dropping out of school would reduce my stress did not understand my need for involvement in activities that promoted recovery.

Completing these classes and managing my life has been facilitated by supportive relationships, engagement in meaningful activities, and access to 14 months of electroconvulsive therapy (ECT) as a last resort for my hard-to-treat depression. ECT affected my short- and long-term memory, with the side effect of cognitive deficiencies that make reading and writing for school challenging and time consuming. I have spent concentrated practice and effort reteaching myself cognitive tasks. ECT, I'm told, "saved" my life. In addition, my medications have played an important role in my recovery. Although medication side effects and psychiatric symptoms created serious difficulties for me, medications, symptom and behavior management, and most importantly, distress/despair tolerance are at the root of my recovery.

Another critical part of recovery is engaging in meaningful activities and having opportunities to learn and grow instead of being treated as a fragile, low functioning individual who is incapable of dealing with stress at any level. I developed an AIDS/STD/HEP-C in SMI program pilot while volunteering at the Department of Social Health Services Austin State Hospital's Adult Psychiatric Services' acute and forensic units. I also enjoy working out, and have rediscovered film and music.

As more consumers with psychiatric disabilities move towards recovery, the culture of persons with mental illness will change to accommodate success. The current culture among persons with mental illness is that of illness and not recovery and fulfillment.

University Shortcomings

At my university, the Services for Students with Disabilities Office (SSD) only seemed to recommend extended times for taking exams and extensions in time for assignments. The disability officer was not cognizant of the types of accommodations a student with a psychiatric disability actually needs or the fact that psychiatric disabilities are episodic and often require repeated requests for accommodations during the course of a semester. I originally was advised not to tell professors the nature of the disability because of the potential for bias and prejudice from faculty. Students with psychiatric disabilities are a marginalized group who often are not identified to faculty or other students because of the discomfort others feel when they are aware of the disability.

A source of stigma from faculty is the perception that students with psychiatric disabilities are receiving "special treatment" when they access accommodations. Some professors are willing to go out of their way to ensure that appropriate accommodations are in place; however, the majority of professors are either too stubborn to change their ways to accommodate invisible disabilities or need training to understand appropriate accommodations to offer (Higher Education, 2003).

I found it necessary to reveal the intimate details of my disability to receive necessary accommodations which was embarrassing for me and appeared to be shocking for the professors. I faced my internalized stigma and fear of rejection when requesting accommodations.

Mental illness affects a student's motivation, concentration, and ability to appropriately engage in social interactions, which are all critical factors in determining academic success. Access to appropriate disability support services plays a key role, enabling students with psychiatric disabilities to remain in and successfully perform in post-secondary education. Section 504 of the Rehabilitation Act of 1973 and the Americans with Disabilities Act of 1990 guarantee the rights of all students with disabilities including those with a psychiatric disability. Post-secondary education is considered necessary to compete in this technological society. Persons with severe mental illness must be able to compete by having access to meaningful employment.

Campus disabilities offices are required by federal law, yet are obscure to students with psychiatric disabilities. There are a growing number of students with psychiatric disabilities on campuses, yet these students are not seeking assistance from disability offices due to fear of exposure and stigma in addition to lack of knowledge about available services by both faculty and students. I believe that campus education about psychiatric disabilities should be given priority status. Accommodations for students with psychiatric disabilities may be complex and require a team approach to identify appropriate accommodations even though there is little to no cost associated with the necessary accommodations.

States do not have specific policies to address issues facing individuals with psychiatric disabilities in post-secondary education; instead states are trying to implement federal policies to comply in order to continue to receive federal funding for all programs. The mental health advocacy communities as well as the state-run mental health systems are focused on access to survival supports like housing and access to medical treatment rather than post-secondary education and quality of life needs for those in recovery. Federal funding has been focused more on work related issues while ignoring assistance for educational attainment that would enable individuals with psychiatric disabilities to reach recovery and obtain post-secondary education necessary to obtain stable employment with benefits and a living wage.

Conclusion

The journey to post-secondary education for many students with psychiatric disabilities has been long and trying. It involves dealing with symptoms, receiving life altering diagnoses, and learning to live with the diagnosis and treatment. Colleges and universities are ill prepared to provide adequate support for these students.

Faculty and students, both with and without psychiatric disabilities, need education on mental illness in order to provide appropriate and consistent reasonable accommodations. Services, when available, often are buried within the general support for students or within the supports for students with physical disabilities. Federal funding tied to psychiatric disabilities is needed.

References

Eudaly, J. (2002). A rising tide: Students with psychiatric disabilities seek services in record numbers. Retrieved November 18, 2005, from The George Washington University Health Resource Center Web site: http://www.heath.gwu.edu/PDFs/Psychiatric%20Disabilities.pdf#xml=http://search.edpolicy.gwu.edu/cgi-bin/texis/webinator/search/xml.txt?query=psychiatric+disabilities&pr=heathsite&prox=page&rorder=500&rprox=500&rdfreq=500&rwfreq=500&rlead=500&sufs=0&order=r&cq=&id=433d559f2.

Higher education: Accommodating post-secondary students with mental illness. (Winter, 2003) *Schizophrenia Digest* [Canadian Edition], 10(1), 28–30. Retrieved November 18, 2005 from York University Counseling and Development Centre Web site: http://www.yorku.ca/cdc/pdp/pdfs/higher_education. PDF

Rogers, S. (2004). Plotting a "Road map to recovery." *Behavioral Health Management*, 24(6), 44–45. Retrieved November 18, 2005 from Academic Research Premier Publication's database.

The stairwell...
represents the risk,
effort, and
awareness that
must be taken,
made or achieved
in order to reach
the skylight.

The stairwell represents a person's life; the dark grey background represents the effects of stigma. The skylight above represents internal and external resources that aid in dispelling the stigma. The light shining through the skylight represents what happens when these resources are allowed to operate; the stigma gets dispelled. The person's true self is allowed to shine. A much more agreeable and appealing picture emerges. The person's life reflects that. However, the stairwell going from bottom to top also represents the risk, effort, and awareness that must be taken, made or achieved in order to reach the skylight.

—Edgar, from *Taking Off the Blinders*, 2005

Soul in Search of Self:
The Lived Experience of Serious Mental Illness

Anonymous

Everything was terribly wrong! My head felt like it was exploding and my body seemed totally foreign — as though it belonged to some tormented stranger. I staggered around my little four-walled concrete room screaming "help me…please, someone,…anyone." I pounded on the locked metal door. There was no reply.

It was 1984. I was 18 years old and was locked away in isolation on a psychiatric ward. I guess I should have seen it coming, but I was just too young to know much about life, much less mental illness.

I had been born to a minister and his wife in the rural farmland of Indiana. I had been wanted and loved. I cherished the church congregation, which my dad led. From the time I could walk, Dad was taking me with him on visits to the sick and elderly.

My mother was attentive and spent hours and hours playing with me, singing to me, and reading. Life was filled with church, pitch-in dinners and kittens in the shed.

From the time I was born I had a special friend named Mr. Lester. We hunted and fished and shopped together as the years went by. Circuses, ice follies, and rodeos were times to enjoy just being with each other.

When I was 4, Mom and Dad and I moved to Aurora, Indiana. There I met lifelong friends, Terri and Lida. Our days were filled with roller skating, swimming, and putting on skits for Mom. Across the street was my dear friend, Marie Schumacher. I remember Chinese checkers, ice milk, and watching Lawrence Welk.

When I was in the sixth grade, I met Nina on the playground as I was surveying the other children on what their favorite type of chewing gum was. When I approached Nina, she let out a big laugh and began to help me with my surveying. She is now a nurse, and she continues to give me a great deal of support and joy. So you see, I did not have a terrible childhood. On the contrary, I had good, solid growing-up years. I was a sensitive child, but my life was well ordered and basically very ordinary. I felt myself to be the apple of many eyes. So it was quite a terrible jolt to my family and me when adolescence hit me with a vengeance.

My teen years were spent crying and feeling like I didn't fit in anywhere. As I look back now, it is easy to realize the crucial mistakes I made. I was eccentric and flamboyant in high school. I did well in drama and felt myself to be so mature and adult that I got early admission to college. I wanted to be where the action was. Little did I know I was on a fast track to nowhere. I thought that being voted "most talented" in high school and receiving a small theatre scholarship at a nearby college was my first stop on my way to fortune and fame.

However once I got to college, I began to feel grossly inadequate in theatre and saw that there were many, many people in the department who were much more talented than I was. I wasn't getting any parts, and I began to retreat from the reality of no longer being the apple of anybody's eye. I went into my own little world and became interested in philosophies of the 1960s. Now instead of being flashily

---

This article was published in the *Psychiatric Rehabilitation Journal* and is reprinted with permission.

overdressed, I became a beatnik. I cared nothing about my appearance and spent all my time reading esoteric books. My parents had to adjust from accepting me taking hours to get my makeup and clothes right to seeing me in wrinkled rags.

It was around this time that I became quite ill and landed in the hospital. As the years went by, I spent quite a lot of my life in different hospitals. My peers were moving on to fulfilling adult roles while I floundered in anguish. I had different symptoms at different times. Sometimes I would be out of my head, and sometimes I just would have a lot of trouble getting along with people. Those years were filled with questioning. I was angry. Everything was wrong. Deep inside nothing seemed to mean anything. I went from deep despair to abject psychosis. Later in my illness I had terrible hallucinations that seemed to make a cesspool and a war zone of my mind—horrible images flickered through my brain that I could not stop.

> I did not have a terrible child-hood....I had good, solid growing-up years....So it was quite a terrible jolt to my family and me when adolescence hit me with a vengeance.

I got no relief, either, from the voices in my head telling me some bad people were going to abduct me and torture me.

At one point, side effects from the medications made my mouth twitch with tardive dyskinesia. For another long period of time (several months) side effects from my medications made my arms flap and I could not stop pacing. I paced in my parents' basement all day, every day. This medication-induced akesthesia was yet another form of living hell. Then I became agoraphobic. I thought some elusive enemy was gassing me through our heating vents. I was truly

paranoid, believing people were poisoning my food and that there were cameras on us all, all the time.

I had an ongoing delusion that lasted many, many years that we were all under surveillance at all times by someone—I did not know if it was the government or organized crime, but I knew that every little mistake I made was being caught on tape and that I had no privacy. I felt invaded upon. Mostly I feared the cameras. Then one day I decided that since everyone was watching, I would try to show the world that I could perform and entertain them. I did a running commentary of events happening in my life to the cameras and spent hours singing and dancing for my observers. I thought I was getting reactions to my performance through the songs that played back to me from the radio. Sometimes I felt my persecutors enjoyed my performance, but mostly they seemed to send me messages about my basic inadequacy.

I know these symptoms must sound quite bizarre to you. However I ask you not to judge me as weird but to realize how painful experiencing these types of symptoms for years really was. After I got better, I had to grieve the oddity and sadness of spending so many years so deluded.

Through all my sufferings I continued to have a faithful pen pal, David. David had heart, humor, and a keen intelligence. We met in a political science class as undergraduates, and we continued to write to each other over the years as I intermittently went in and out of hospitals. On December 17, 1994, I called David to wish him a Merry Christmas. It was the day I picked up the pay phone on the psych unit where I had been for over 2 months. David was completing his second Master's degree and was glad to hear from me.

In the 2 months I had been at the Community Mental Health Center in Lawrenceburg, Indiana, I had gotten excellent treatment. With the help of my wonderful psychiatrist, Dr. Kelly, I finally got on the right dosage of medication. The new psychotropic drugs like the one I take, Clozaril, are truly miracle medications. With good medicine, good treatment, and time to heal in the hospital, I started to really get better. After 3 months of therapeutic activities in the hospital—psycho-educational groups, reading self-help books from the unit's library and journaling, I was ready to move to a group home. The coordinator of the group home, Bill Hardy, was kind enough to let me stay at the group home because I was scared to go back to living by myself at my apartment. At the group home, I felt safe and cared for. One helper, Lois, was particularly special to me as she took me to church with her. This was a time of healing and simplicity.

Every night at the group home, David would call me on the hallway payphone. He did not seem to be bothered or deterred by my illness at all. I remember driving up to see him for the first time in years. We delighted in each other's company and spent hours on his computer, walking in the park, and watching old movies together. It was a happy and nurturing time in my life. I hadn't felt so happy and blessed since I had been a little kid.

The greatest gift I ever gave myself was to hook up with David. We got married on May 25, 1996. It was the best thing that had ever happened to me. Overcoming my schizoaffective disorder and his muscular dystrophy seemed easy—we were in love. Our parents were thrilled to see us so happy together and both sets of parents showered us with love and kindness. Daniel Fisher and Laurie Ahern talk in their writings about how close, trusting relationships are vital to recovery. It is crucial to have someone who believes in you and sees the good in you and will never give up on you. David made me feel safe. I have always trusted him completely. Because he battles a physical illness, he understands what it is to wrestle with disability. His patience and acceptance of his limitations are that of a Zen master (which he reads a lot about). He has been a phenomenal role model. He is always car-

> **It is crucial to have someone who believes in you and sees the good in you and will never give up on you.**

ing, and accepts and loves me with all my foibles. When I am breaking, he has strong arms to lift me up.

Fall of 1997 was another special time for me. I got a job at Clermont Counseling Center working with persons like myself who had a mental illness. It was unbelievably rewarding to finally find an environment where I felt I really fit in and could do some productive work. Work is very therapeutic when one finds an environment that is nurturing and that allows for creativity, control, and personal growth. Working in the mental health field is especially rewarding because one can begin to make good use of one's past suffering. I began to feel my life had great meaning and purpose as I reached beyond myself to help others. About a year ago, my fantastic boss, Anne Combs, asked me if I would be willing to go public with the fact that I have a mental illness. It was scary, but I decided to go for it. It has been very rewarding to be honest and forthright about who I am and what I've been through.

> **I began to feel my life had great meaning and purpose as I reached beyond myself to help others.**

Currently I am developing a new position at Clermont Counseling Center called Coordinator of Consumer Affairs. I lead a peer support group named Team Achieve where we support one another, are active politically in mental health issues, and speak publicly to help destigmatize mental illness. Our message is that we can fit in and contribute to society, that with the new meds and proper psychosocial rehabilitation, we can be good neighbors and even gift the world with the compassion we have learned through our suffering. The newer atypical antipsychotic medications produced sleep and reduction of symptoms, and I consider them the first wave of my healing. My second wave of healing came when I took a part-time clerical job at a library. I was proud to be able to work again, even if for only a few hours a week. Sometimes I would think people were laughing at me, and I had setbacks, but I went home and rested and showed up the next time I was scheduled to work. My resilience gradually grew. My progress was slow–a series of small successes interspersed with little stresses and setbacks.

It is a big ego boost to work in the mental health field after watching professionals so admiringly from the patient's perspective. Becoming a case management aide made me feel I had crossed over some crucial threshold. I was intensely proud of my job and tried diligently to do good work. Feelings of self-efficiency began to surface. My third wave of healing was built on the strong foundation of having created a remarkable support system for myself. I work hard to nurture my relationships with friends and family. Being totally accepted and secure at home, I was free to build my career. As I went public with my illness, I gradually became less and less ashamed. When I began having opportunities to do public speaking, I finally recaptured the joy I'd had years before in doing theater. I found that I had matured and was a better speaker and writer than I had been before my illness struck.

I am working on my second Master's degree at UC in Community Counseling. It feels good to set educational goals and achieve them. I have had a lot of "ah-ha" moments as I learned which of my behaviors stemmed from my mental illness. This knowledge has helped me to be more confident. I have learned to do something I had never done before—celebrate my successes. I find it helpful to make lists, to prioritize my activities. I find organizing my environment uplifting. I also use self-care techniques of working on not being so self-critical or perfectionistic. I have learned to go easier on myself, accept who I am, and be okay with me—flaws, scars, and all. I have learned to value what is on the inside of others and myself. I have matured to a point where I can see the positive in others and myself. Immersing myself in recovery literature helped make this possible.

As my confidence grew, I learned to be authentic and have become much better at expressing uncomfortable feelings. But I still have a tendency to sit on feelings until I get home and then "let it all out" with great intensity to David. He accepts this with equanimity, but I'm hoping to improve in my ability to express my true feelings as I'm experiencing them.

My focus in life now is on wellness, a healthy spirituality, continued growth, and helping others. I have a supportive family, a beloved and revered husband, a home, and Dusky Sky–my dog. I have a strong support system of friends that sustain me—Erin, Valerie, Vicki, Anne T., Terri, and Nina. I also feel very strong ties and support from the consumers I work with. They are truly a blessing. Educating myself about mental illness and self-help possibilities has enlightened me and helped me cope more effectively at work, and helped me to view my illness as a small part of me I need to manage, as someone with diabetes has to manage his or her life. I no longer cringe when people use words like "chronic" or "psychotic," because my entire personhood is no longer grounded in the disgrace those terms once engendered in me. The downhill escalation of my schizo affective disorder has been arrested. Once that happened, I began to feel I had some semblance of control over my life, and this transformed me into a much more hopeful person who could be excited about her future.

> I have learned to go easier on myself, accept who I am, and be okay with me—flaws, scars, and all.

The final wave of my healing has coalesced with my building of a peer support program at Clermont Counseling Center. I share the eye-opening enthusiasm of possibilities for persons with chronic mental illness because of the influx of information on role recovery our agency has been given access to by consultants from the Boston Center for Psychiatric Rehabilitation. Sharing the joy, hope, and wholeness of these materials with my peers has been a catalyst to creating a synergistic community of empowered consumers motivated to fight stigma, be politically active, and to raise the level of compassion in society. We are building on one another's enthusiasm. We are ecstatic to shed the role of passive, dependent patient in favor of a vibrant, heroic psychiatric survivor who has much to give others. We have been stifled for too long. Being able to help others like ourselves to put meaning into their lives has moved us exponentially up the positive rungs of the self-efficacy continuum.

> I now direct my own recovery and take great joy in meaningful relationships and work.

I have stopped apologizing for myself. I now see myself as a human being who can say yes to life and make important decisions for myself. I now direct my own recovery and take great joy in meaningful relationships and work. I can make a difference in my community and have the courage to do so. I believe in myself and am now strong enough to overcome negative beliefs with the encouragement of my support system. I can freely love and be loved. The greatest joy I have is facilitating the discovery of what recovery can mean in the lives of the people I encounter. Seeing people released from the bondage of shame and hopelessness is deeply gratifying. I rise with my peers to make the world a healthier place where respect and dignity flourish. Never give up. No life is beyond regeneration.

We can bury
stigma forever.

photovoice

I see an archway beneath a bright sun. It's the entrance to a graveyard: "The Graveyard for Discontinued Ice Cream Flavors" at the Ben and Jerry's factory in Vermont. All things pass, everything changes. Just as Ben and Jerry found a way to dispose of discontinued flavors, we too can find a way to dispose of discontinued labels. We can be more visible in our society; we can build relationships with so called "normal" people; we can make ourselves heard. We still may have to put up with stigmatization of our disabilities, but this can and will change. We can bury stigma forever.

—Derek, from *Taking Off the Blinders,* 2005

Open Doors

John S. Caswell

Hello, my name is John. I have a 17-year history of drug and alcohol abuse but gave up drugs and alcohol in 1987. I since have been diagnosed with a mental health disorder, "chronic paranoid schizophrenia." Although I had experienced a psychotic episode in 1979 and found myself on the mental health ward a number of times following my first episode, it was not until 1990 that I was diagnosed with schizophrenia, three years after giving up drugs and alcohol.

When an individual is diagnosed with a mental health disorder, it is the whole life of the individual that has become disordered. Severe mental illness most often affects every aspect of the individual's life, including but not limited to, housing, employment and finances, personal and social relationships, and one's ability to carry out the daily activities necessary to take care of oneself. Having been diagnosed with a severe mental illness, I was eligible to receive payments through our federal government and the Social Security Disability Insurance program because I was unable to work and support myself. Shortly after being assigned my "mental health label," I left the New England area to live with my brother and his family in Salt Lake City, Utah.

The house in Salt Lake was rather small, so I slept in the camper trailer in the back yard. My brother drank alcohol and would, from time to time, invite friends into his home to party. I was trying to stay clean so most of my time was spent in the camper.

Although there was a television in the camper and I did a lot of reading, I was having very little interaction with other people. Oh, I would go into the house two or three times a day, but the people there were always the same, unless there was a party going on. It began to seem as if each day was the same as the day before. I felt what I needed was to see new faces and to interact with different people. After all, we humans are by nature, social beings.

I soon found myself going out to the bars with my brother and his friends. At first I would just drink juice and I was in fact, for a time, their designated driver. But before long I started going to the bars alone, and eventually reached a point in which I thought it would be okay to drink "just one beer." As those of us who share this problem with alcohol know, one beer is too many and a dozen are not enough. Within three months I found that I was facing a driving while intoxicated charge.

When I went to court I told the judge that I was guilty as charged, and that I should have known better than to drink and drive. I was ordered to pay a fine and to perform 40 hours of community service. I had refused to take an alcohol sensor test the night I had been arrested, therefore my license was suspended for a year. I paid the fine and performed the community service. I also attended the impaired driver education course that was required to get my license back, although it would be a year before driving would be a reality for me. Then I flew home to New England.

This article was published in the *Psychiatric Rehabilitation Journal*, 2003, 27(2), 191–197, and is reprinted with permission. Open Doors also was published in Caswell, J.S. (2008). *Learning curve*. West Lebanon, NH: Granite Steps Publications.

I could not afford an apartment of my own when I first returned to New England, so I moved in with two other people. One of the individuals I lived with would, from time to time, drink alcohol and although they knew of my problem, they kept it in the house. This was very hard for me. After all, although I was in the process of recovery from a 17-year history of substance abuse and had managed to stay clean for three years, I had recently relapsed into alcohol. As you have already read, that relapse ended in a very bad way.

Trying to give up alcohol while living with someone who drinks is not easy. It seemed as if each time I opened the refrigerator to get a glass of milk or a snack, I would be confronted with the temptation of alcohol. There was also one cupboard in the apartment where I had discovered a stash of hard liquor. After learning of the stash, I never opened that cupboard door again. The temptation was very hard to deal with, but I somehow managed to overcome. Each time I was confronted with the temptation of alcohol, I made a conscious decision and/or choice not to drink. I had finally learned where "just one drink" could lead and I had had enough. I was determined not to give in.

> When an individual is diagnosed with a mental health disorder it is the whole life of the individual that has become disordered.

The mood swing of people who drink can be very unpredictable even during times when they haven't been drinking. This is rather hard to explain but can be understood by those of us who have had the personal experience of living with an individual who drinks. I never knew what type of mood the individual I was living with would be when they came through the door so I made it a point to be in my room before they came home from work. I sometimes refer to this as "self-imposed isolation" but in reality, I was isolating for reasons that at the time were beyond my control.

Another fact that needs to be considered in regard to my isolation is that I was taking the antipsychotic medication Haldol. Haldol helped with some of the symptoms of my mental illness (schizophrenia); however, I always felt a little "disconnected," "out of sorts," and "paranoid" while taking it. Therefore, I didn't like to be around other people. I was afraid I would do something out of the ordinary or that I would upset someone.

Although I had reconnected with our local mental health agency and had tried to the best of my ability, I just couldn't land a job. The guilt I experienced through knowing that other members of the household went to work each day while I was in fact unemployed is another reason I would go to my room before they came home from work. I began to experience guilt over the fact that I was receiving a check from the government when, in fact, I was unemployed. The more I thought about these things, the more depressed I became and the more I isolated.

As I have already stated, we humans are, by nature, social beings. We live to have contact, personal interaction, and to share "new life experiences" with other beings of our kind. The isolation I was experiencing may in some ways be similar to that experienced by an individual who is in prison. My bedroom had, in fact, become my prison, and I had sentenced myself to solitary confinement.

I don't know if an individual in solitary confinement is allowed to write or read, but if not, what is there to live for? If not allowed to read, the only thing the individual has to live for are memories of the past and the hope that one day soon the isolation will end. Early on in the period of isolation I had experienced while in Salt Lake City, I had been able to find comfort in reading; however, during this period, the thought of reading didn't even enter my mind.

As time passed and I continued to isolate, I began to think of the things that had led up to my isolation. I didn't think of the person I lived with who kept alcohol in the house, but rather of my past use of drugs and alcohol and of past misdeeds I had commit-

> Isolation can lead to depression simply by the lack of contact and interaction with other human beings.

ted. This too contributed to the depression and isolation I was experiencing. I began to believe that I was undeserving and unworthy of meaningful relationships with others.

The solitary confinement I was experiencing was different than that experienced by an individual in prison. I was able to leave my room and, in fact, was afforded all the rights and freedoms of any citizen of our great nation who abides by our laws and respects the rights of others. Through circumstances that I thought were beyond my control, I had restricted myself from exercising these basic rights and freedoms.

Another difference is that there was a television in the apartment, and early on, I would leave my room and watch television while other members of our household were at work. Television can help alleviate feelings of isolation, as can radio, but these are just a temporary fix, in effect a Band-Aid for an ailment that only can be overcome through personal interaction with others and the sharing of new life experiences. After all, have you ever noticed how many reruns are played on television? And if you watch the news on television or listen to it on the radio, it can become rather depressing. Although from time to time the news does report a story with a positive outcome, seldom is there a report that helps one to continue to have faith in human nature.

Isolation can lead to depression simply by the lack of contact and interaction with other human beings. This was the 20th century. Most people who could afford a telephone owned one. Through the telephone people are able to communicate with other members of their community, but as I began to isolate, I was forced to call the same people over and over again. And because most of my old friends still used drugs and alcohol, there were very few people whom I could call. This is due solely to the fact that I was isolating

and, thereby, not creating for myself the opportunity to meet new people and share new life experiences. Early on, before I was deep into my isolation, I couldn't wait to call friends and learn of new and exciting things that were going on in their life. While isolating I seldom had much to contribute to the conversation simply because I was not experiencing anything new and exciting myself. When asked about my day or life, I often reported, "Oh, just another day," or "Nothing new," then I would go on to ask, "What's up with you?" As the isolation become more intense, I reached a point in which I stopped calling my friends altogether. I was unaware I had done this.

Finding myself trapped in this "prison of isolation," I eventually reached a point at which I couldn't help but think of "breaking free" and/or "putting an end to it." This had just become too much. There has to be more to life than this. I began to realize that what I needed was to find a way to somehow create and experience some degree of continual change that included sharing new life experiences with other people.

So how was I able to "break free" and begin to feel comfortable outside of my prison and out in the community? I was very lucky in that at the time there was an F. W. Woolworth store located in the city about five miles from my home. When the isolation reached a point at which I could no longer stand it, I left my room, took a shower, dressed in warm clothes because it was winter, and took the bus to the city. Once there, I stood in front of the Woolworth store and, as people entered or exited the store, I held the door open for them. Most people would thank me for doing this. Shortly after starting this act of kindness, I began to take notice of and count each time someone said "Thank you" to me. I also made a point of saying, "You're welcome." When I needed a break from the winter weather, I would go to the coffee shop in Woolworth's and have a cup of coffee. In taking those breaks, I got to know the people who were working behind the counter of the coffee shop as well as some of the customers. I never mentioned the fact that I was their doorman, but if I recall correctly, others may have brought up the subject once or twice.

I'm not sure what I felt while holding the door open on that first day, but I can't help but to think that hearing the words, "thank you" repeatedly throughout the day helped me to begin to change. In the beginning I would just say, "You're welcome" as people gave me thanks, but eventually I also would smile and say, "Have a great day!"

With the approach of spring, I had reached a point at which I would go to Woolworth's and hold the doors open almost every weekday. I was no longer trapped in my self-imposed prison; I had "broken free." I now had purpose and meaning in my life. I was contributing to society and bringing at least a little joy to my fellow human beings. I now had a reason to leave my room, and I began to feel better about myself. If I took a day off from opening the doors, when I returned to Woolworth's, people would ask where I had been. This too contributed to my wellness because I began to feel as though people missed and cared about me.

> Recovery is a journey, not a destination.
> For me, recovery is a state of being, a feeling of sustainable wellness and continuous growth.

I believe it was April of that year when our local mental health agency secured the cleaning contract with the local research and engineering laboratory. I gave up my doorman's job and went to work as a custodian.

Although I really didn't like the type of employment that I now found myself doing, I did, in fact, begin to feel better about myself because I now was employed. I had been told by people who work for the mental health agency that this would be a temporary position, but they did not put any limits on the length of time I would be allowed to work for them. Although my vocational counselor had told me that she thought I could pass the GED test and had encouraged me to take it, at the time I had very little confidence in my ability and kept coming up with excuses as to why I wouldn't take the test. Once I started work as a custodian, I don't believe she mentioned the test again until after I quit my job.

When I started working as a custodian, I worked four hours a day, five days a week. I was told that I was working over what our Social Security Administration considered to be "Substantial Gainful Activity," and if I continued to do so, I would lose my Social Security Disability check. This did not concern me because there was a new building being built at work, and I would be allowed to work full-time when the building was complete. When the building was completed, I started working full-time and soon thereafter became the lead person. My new duties included giving support and encouragement to other consumer/employees and making sure the work got done when someone was out sick.

It seemed that there was at least one person out almost every day. In the beginning I didn't mind this because I had no problem filling in for individuals who were out. The problem began when my boss went on vacation. When the other employees learned the boss was going to be out, they started taking time off. They didn't understand that he would learn how much time they had taken off when he returned from vacation. During the ten workdays he was away, I had to cover fourteen shifts in which people had taken time off and repeated shifts for one person who had, in fact, quit her job. As this was my first experience as a supervisor, I took it upon myself to do the work of others when they were out. I had yet to learn to delegate and share responsibility.

I still was taking the antipsychotic medication Haldol and, in fact, with the support and guidance of my doctor was in the process of reducing my dose. At one point I had been taking 10 mg per day, but because of the side effects, I had only taken it intermittently. I just couldn't stand the side effects. With the assistance of my doctor, I reduced my dose to 5 mg and may have even gone as low as 2½, although the total amount I reduced has slipped from my memory. While taking the full dose, I believe I had been meeting with my doctor every month, but as we reduced my dose, I began meeting with him once every three months. Although while taking 10 mg I had taken it only intermittently, while reducing my dose I took it as prescribed.

Things had gone well at work for a while, but when my boss had taken vacation and all those people took time off, I began to feel overwhelmed and reached a point in which I hated going to work. I never knew how many people would be out sick.

Although I don't remember when the conversation took place, at one point during my employment journey, I had told my supports manager I wanted to give up my job and go to college and become a substance abuse counselor. I don't at this time remember what her response had been, but I remember it to have been very discouraging, so I didn't mention it again, to anyone.

When I started work as a custodian I felt a little better about myself because I was employed and was, in fact, contributing to my household. I was surviving without my SSDI check, and I was contributing to my community, but although I had been taking an anti-depressant, I was still experiencing depression and it was now intensifying.

My living situation had not changed, and I continued to isolate while at home. I was taking the bus to work because I didn't own a car. I was trying to save money for a car and, in fact, bought one for $650 only to learn it would cost about $900 to get it through inspection. I sold the car for $300 and continued to take the bus to work. The bus was seldom on schedule, and it seemed that I was always waiting for it. To insure I arrived at work on time, I took the early bus and usually report-

> When I started work...I felt a little better about myself because I was employed and was in fact contributing to my household.

ed to work about half an hour early. Reliable transportation would have been helpful.

Another aspect of my life in which a car would have been helpful is that I'm divorced and have two children who lived about 25 miles from my home. Although their mother brought them to town from time to time so they could visit and my mother had on occasion picked them up, it was seldom that they got to see their dad. When we did get to see each other, I really didn't know how to act. I was experiencing side effects of my medication and I was depressed. Although I tried to the best of my ability to act like a "normal person and dad," I do not believe I was very successful at this. I felt very guilty because I was behind in my child support payment and over the fact that my children seldom had the opportunity to spend time with their dad. I also missed them.

The day came in which my mother gave me a ride to pick up my children for a visit, and although I had called before leaving my apartment and learned that their phone was no longer in service, we made the drive. I was concerned about my children. When we arrived at their home I found the house to be empty. They had moved.

It took about three months to locate them at which time I learned they were living in a state located about 2,000 miles away. After learning their phone number, I called their home. My ex-wife asked how I had found their number and why I was calling. Over the years she most often would ask why I had called each time I tried to get in touch with our children. Although I called often, they did not have an answering machine and had no way of knowing that I was trying to get in touch with them. It was rare that we had an opportunity to speak with one another. I wrote letters and did, in fact, receive a few in return, but we eventually stopped writing. I mailed each of my children self-addressed, stamped postcards at the suggestion of my supports manager; to the best of my knowledge they still have them. I sent them cameras and film and have yet to receive my first picture. I asked my ex-wife to send me copies of their report cards, and she sent a few, but this too eventually ended. I had tried to the best of my ability to build a meaningful relationship with my children, and I didn't know what else I could do short of moving to the state in which they now lived. I was learning the difficulty of trying to maintain a long-distance relationship and it just wasn't working. During this time they had moved again, and there was a time in which we had no contact; therefore, after finally getting in touch with them again, it took time to reestablish our relationship. All of these things were being mulled repeatedly in my mind, and I became very depressed and confused.

> My mind was full of all the reasons for which I wanted to end my life and the thoughts played over and over.

During the time my doctor and I were in the process of cutting down my medication, I had a lot of Haldol in my bedroom. I'm not sure, but because my income was low, I may have been granted a scholarship from the pharmaceutical company. I do know that at one point I did, in fact, have a scholarship and was receiving my medication in bottles of 100 tablets.

Upon arriving home from a very hard day of work, I had just had enough. I went to my bedroom and got my medication. Then I went to the kitchen sink, filled a glass with water, and attempted suicide by overdosing on Haldol. I'm not sure how many pills I took, but I guess the number to be around 150. Then I went back into my bedroom and tried to go to sleep, but I couldn't. My mind was full of all the reasons for which I wanted to end my life and the thoughts played over and over.

As the night progressed I thought more about my children and mother and how my suicide would affect them. I eventually reached a point in which I felt guilty about attempting to take my life. I no longer wanted to die, but the effects of the Haldol were beginning to take their toll. My sinuses were so dry that I was afraid they would split open, my head hurt, my stomach was upset, all of my muscles ached, and my entire body felt strange. It seemed as if my mind was disconnected from my body. I no longer wanted to die, but I didn't want the people I was living with to know I had attempted suicide so I stayed in my room until I was sure they had gone to sleep for the night. While I was waiting, I felt terrible over what I had done.

I think it was around midnight that I left my room, walked downtown, and called a taxi. When the taxi arrived, I asked the driver to take me to the hospital. As we approached the hospital the driver asked if I wanted to go to the main entrance or the emergency room. I asked him to drop me off at the main entrance.

When we arrived, I got out of the taxi, entered the hospital, and sort of paced in the main lobby. Before long I started to hear a familiar sound. Someone was vacuuming the hall. As time passed, the sound became louder and louder, and before I knew it, a custodian came around the corner with a vacuum cleaner that was the same brand and color as those I use at work. This was just too much. I left the hospital and sat down on a bench out front. While outside I smoked a couple of cigarettes and vomited twice. Then I went back into the hospital, called a taxi, and went home.

The next day was Friday. I did not go to work. I just didn't want to face any people. I felt physically ill, and I was still upset emotionally. I felt terribly guilty. After the people I was living with went to work, I went upstairs and paced in one of the bedrooms. I went downstairs before they came home and went out on the back porch and smoked a cigarette. There was a note from two of my counselors stuck to the door.

They had stopped by because they were concerned that I had not called in sick and had not shown up for work. I had never done that before.

I spent most of the weekend in my bedroom, and on Monday I met with my doctor and the person who oversaw the custodians. I told them I wanted to quit my job and go to college and become a counselor. They told me that rather than give up my job I could take a leave of absence, and they would hold my job for me. While discussing this, I eventually had to tell them that they just didn't understand that I didn't want to work as a custodian any longer. I had been employed as a custodian for two and a half years, although at the start of my employment, I had been told that the job would be temporary.

A short time following my suicide attempt I told my doctor I had overdosed by taking 150 tablets of Haldol the Thursday night before I quit my job. If I recall correctly his response was that if it had been a different medication, I might not have been able to tell him about the overdose. I don't believe we ever discussed the reason for the overdose nor do I recall him recommending that I see a therapist.

Following my suicide attempt, my doctor put me on the newer antipsychotic medication, Risperdal, and it seems to work rather well, although in times of stress I have to increase my dose. I have not attempted to take my life since changing medication in 1995.

When my vocational counselor learned that I wanted to go to college, she told me the first step would be to get my GED. I told her I had just quit my job and that I had no money. She was able to get the mental health agency to pay for the test. When I told her I had no way to get to the testing facility she said she would give me a ride. True to her word, she brought me to the testing facility, both nights that it took me to complete the required tests. She did this although the tests were held at night after her regular work hours and in spite of the fact that it snowed both nights. I took the test in December of 1995 and learned of the results in January of '96. I had passed the test.

> When my vocational counselor learned that I wanted to go to college, she told me the first step would be to get my GED.

Another thing my vocational counselor did for me was to connect me with the State of New Hampshire Department of Vocational Rehabilitation (voc rehab). My voc rehab counselor had me take a vocational assessment to learn if my career choice would be a good match and/or fit. When I got the results of the assessment, I learned that a career in human services would, in fact, be a good match for me. When I left the voc rehab office that day, I took it upon myself to walk directly across the mall and take the elevator to the office of Lebanon College.

When I walked into the office, I asked the receptionist if the college was offering any courses in English. I was told that a course in English grammar would be offered the next semester. I also was informed that the course would cost $235. When I told her I had no money, she let me know that the Greater Lebanon Chamber of Commerce was just starting a scholarship program and she gave me an application. I filled out the application and wrote the required essay. Then I mailed the application and essay to the Chamber of Commerce. The essay I wrote is titled, "Why I Want to Become a Substance Abuse Counselor" and is published in my book, "Reflections of Reality."

Within a very short time, I was invited into the Chamber office for an interview. By the end of the interview, I had learned that I soon would receive a letter from the Chamber that would explain their decision in regard to my scholarship. Very shortly after that, I received a letter with an enclosed check for $200. I paid the remaining $35 for the course and $15 for the required workbook. I passed that course with a grade of A-.

In taking that first college course and in doing so on my own initiative, I think I was able to prove to my voc rehab counselor that I was serious in respect to my educational goal. After sharing my grade with him, he asked if I would like to attend a more challenging school. I welcomed the opportunity, and he paid for a course in critical thinking at the College for Lifelong Learning (CLL).

During the time that I took my first college course, I moved into an apartment the mental health agency used as transitional housing. The apartment was close enough to Lebanon College that I could walk to class. When I stated attending CLL, I arranged for a taxi to pick me up both before and after class.

I think there was only one night in which the taxi didn't pick me up for class. That night I walked. The problem was getting home, not only on that night, but on other nights as well. One night my instructor gave me a ride home. Another night after standing in the cold, dark, snowy parking lot for better than half an hour waiting for my taxi, I accepted a ride home from a lady who had driven by, seen me standing there and turned around to see that I was okay. There were also a number of nights in which I had to walk home after class. I passed that course with a grade of B.

> Although it is important not to dwell on the past, it is equally important to come to terms with it and to keep it in perspective.

Next my voc rehab counselor had me apply for student loans and register for classes with New Hampshire Technical Institute (NHTI), located in Concord, NH some 65 miles south of my home in Lebanon. I was able to register with the college through the mail, and my mother agreed to give me a ride to Concord for orientation because I did not own a car. It was on the way home from Concord that my mother told me how proud of me she is.

My voc rehab counselor told me the State of NH would not pay for a car for me, so I went back to work as a custodian. In three months time, I was able to save about $1000 and buy a used car. Voc rehab paid my car insurance, bought my books and supplies, and paid some of my tuition.

During the time I was taking the class at Lebanon College, but before I moved into the apartment owned by the mental health agency, a couple of friends stopped by and asked if I would be willing to help them move some furniture. The furniture was to be used for a Peer Support Center in Lebanon. I helped them load a U-haul truck with furniture donated by Dartmouth College. Then we unloaded the truck at a friend's house.

By the time I was able to buy a car, Next Step, our Peer Support Center, had been open for a while and I began to stop in. In the beginning, I was rather quiet and would stay at the center for only a few minutes, but eventually, I began to share positive things about my educational journey and spend more time there. As I began to get to know people, I also shared my poetry, and in doing so, they learned I was receiving services through the local mental health agency. They also learned that I was in the process of recovery from a history of substance abuse.

Through Next Step I began to meet people who had been through and were sharing life experiences similar to those I had experienced. It was through this sharing that I began to feel that I was not alone. I was overcoming my substance abuse and had been clean for a number of years, and the more I shared, the more comfortable I felt. It also seemed the more I was willing to share, the more others shared about themselves. Members of Next Step did not judge me for my past use of drugs and alcohol or my mental illness, but I believe they may have been impressed by the fact that I was overcoming my past and even attending college. I began to feel accepted as well as respected.

While attending the Technical Institute, I had an opportunity to move into an apartment that is not considered transitional and have lived there for four years. I do not allow alcohol in my home or my car, and I try not to put myself in vulnerable situations where people are drinking. I have not had a drink of alcohol since before leaving Salt Lake City, and October of 2002 marked twelve years of clean time for me.

About midway through my educational journey, the mental health agency assigned a new vocational counselor to work with me. She was a great support during the rest of my educational journey. We also traveled to Concord to attend the State Benefits Planners Meetings, and together, we became quite knowledgeable in both Federal and State benefits. She was also a great support as I started working at our peer support center at a time in which the center experienced a number of leadership changes. She also supported and assisted other members of the center in many ways.

In May of 2000, I graduated from New Hampshire Technical Institute with high honors and an Associates Degree in Human Services with Specialization in Alcohol and Drug Abuse Counseling. I am currently employed as a Peer Support Specialist with Next Step and have been working in that capacity for over two years.

> I like to believe I'm "opening doors" that will allow others to move forward in their journey of recovery and assist them in improving their quality of life.

Through our Peer Support Center I have found a place where I feel safe, welcome, accepted and respected, as well as challenged. I also can rest assured that I will continue to receive the support I need as I face new life challenges. This is evident in the genuine, sincere support I received when I told the Next Step community of my most recent challenge, a diagnosis that I have been infected with the Hepatitis C Virus.

With the assistance of one of our members, I was able to develop my own Wellness Recovery Action Plan based on the work of Mary Ellen Copeland. I don't look at my plan every day, but I do from time to time review and revise it as I become more self-aware and learn of more effective coping strategies.

A year after starting work with Next Step, I wrote a paper titled "How Peer Support Can Work for You." Although I believe each of us is entitled to our own definition of Peer Support, I sometimes share my paper with new members to sort of give them a baseline for defining how peer support can work for them. The paper is posted on the wall of the center and I feel good about that. I have contributed something that hopefully will live on long after my journey as I now know it is over.

I continue to open doors for others and I make a point of saying "You're welcome" as they give me thanks. I also try to remember to say "Thank you" to people who show me acts of kindness. And I have written a poem titled "My Thank You Bank" that I have published in my book, "Reflections of Reality."

A while ago I told my supports manager that my recovery could have progressed faster and more smoothly had I had a therapist on my team. At that time he asked if I would like a therapist now. I told him I had made it this far without one and that I would think about it. The subject has been re-explored with my new supports manager. To the best of my knowledge, this is the eighth supports manager I've been assigned since 1991 when I reconnected with our local mental health agency.

Although it is important not to dwell on the past, it is equally important to come to terms with it and to keep it in perspective. I am coming to terms with my past by writing about it and sharing my writing with other people. I am able to do this through our Peer Support Center where I am accepted and respected for the person I have become, as opposed to being judged for a past that I am not particularly proud of.

I'm now experiencing a richer, fuller life that is better and beyond that which I had become accustomed to while caught up in the world of addictions, isolation, depression, and early recovery. Through our Peer Support Center, I share my life with others in hope that they too may meet and overcome challenges that are similar to those I have overcome. I like to believe I'm "opening doors" that will allow others to move forward in their journey of recovery and assist them in improving their quality of life.

Today, thanks to our Peer Support Center, my life includes many meaningful personal and social relationships and the sharing of numerous "new life experiences." For this I am extremely grateful.

Recovery is a journey, not a destination. For me, recovery is a state of being, a feeling of sustainable wellness and continuous growth.

CHAPTER 2

Increasing Knowledge and Control

Recovery: The Heart and Soul of Treatment

Wilma Townsend & Nicole Glasser

Everyone has a journey, each with its own chasms and perils along the way. For some a mental illness becomes their chasm. Certainly it is a difficult one to bear: the devastation of mental illnesses can be plain to see (the majority of people who have a mental illness are unrecognizable from the rest of society)—people may lose jobs, friends, places to live, and educational opportunities—but solutions can be found. Finding hope can be the beacon, the guiding light that can make everything possible, that can reawaken dreams once thought dormant, or recreate a life anew.

At root, recovery is about the stories of individuals because each person's journey is unique and special. In the early 1980s the Ohio Department of Mental Health created a fund for peer-run services as a means to help people move beyond illness. With $10,000 a peer-run drop-in center was opened in Cincinnati. I had the opportunity to see first-hand how this project changed the lives of the individuals involved. It was then I decided on the power and potential of recovery and to do more work on the concept.

What Is Recovery

Recovery is about refusing to settle for less. Imagine if a person with a broken leg was called recovered if they were pain free, yet they still could not walk. Instead of focusing primarily on symptom relief, as the medical model dictates, recovery casts a much wider spotlight on restoration of self-esteem, identity and on attaining meaningful roles in society (Deegan, 1996). These are the things that everyone in recovery needs in order to walk again. Recovery is a process by which an individual recovers self-esteem, dreams, self-worth, pride, choice, dignity and meaning: this is the recipe for mental health, the perfect antidote for mental "illness."

Recovery is variously called a process, an outlook, a vision, and a guiding principle. There is neither a single agreed-upon definition of recovery nor a single way to measure it. But the overarching message is that hope and restoration of a meaningful life are possible, despite serious mental illnesses (Deegan, 1988; Anthony, 1993; Stocks, 1995; Spaniol & Zipple, 1997). In fact, hope is recognized unanimously as one of the most important determinants of recovery (Fisher, 1996; Lovejoy, 1982; Orrin, 1997; Weingarten, 1994; Russinova, 1998). Moreover, clinicians who embrace the importance of hope and help to instill it in others also are embracing a deeper truth—that people can heal, that people can change, that people can rise up against life's deepest of chasms.

Recovery does not imply full recovery, in which full ability is restored and no medications are needed. Moreover, recovery will not necessarily go in one orderly direction, sometimes steps forward will be followed by steps back. These steps back need not be interpreted as failure. Relapse can be a part of the overall recovery process. For example, hospitalization, rather than a failure or hopeless backtracking,

This article was published in the *Psychiatric Rehabilitation Journal*, 2003, 27(1), 83–86, and is reprinted with permission.

can instead be viewed as an opportunity to learn. Service providers can then work with the consumer and address such questions as "What happened?" "How did it happen?" and "What can we do to be better prepared for these symptoms in the future?" Without this learning from the symptoms and acute crises of illnesses, people will not have the opportunity to move on with their lives; instead they will be stuck with the same symptoms and crises happening over and over. Everyday clinicians can help people in this learning process by having conversations with them about what they are going through, what they can do differently, and when symptoms worsen what they need to do for themselves. In this way, every setback and every symptom can actually pave the way towards recovery.

> Finding hope can be the beacon, the guiding light that can make everything possible...

Moreover, this level of conversation only can happen if there is a relationship built. "It is imperative that we teach students/clinicians that personal relationship is the most powerful tool they have in working with people" (Deegan, 1996).

Recovery also can be said to be a personal process of overcoming the negative impact of a psychiatric disability despite its continued presence. In addition to symptoms, people will face additional internal and external obstacles. Internal obstacles are those things related to oneself, such as internalized discriminatory attitudes, feeling helpless, low self-esteem, fear of failure, and lack of support. External obstacles are those things that cannot be controlled such as societal stigma, loss of job, loss of housing, and loss of family and friends. The external obstacles impact people twice as hard, yet the system is not always set up in a way to deal with the external issues. The only way for a system to be recovery-focused is by recognizing and addressing both the external and internal obstacles. It is these disabilities and disadvantages, after all, which can combine to limit a person's recovery even when one has become predominantly asymptomatic (Anthony, 1993).

Recovery is also about embracing people's humanity. Curtis (2000) describes this as the deciphering between the *me* and *it*. The me is the person, the it is the illness. People identifying themselves as an illness is a sure way of helping them believe that illness is the end all in their life. Alternately, by looking at the me in the equation, one can instead focus on the entire person, making it easier to focus on a person's assets and strengths. Looking at the whole person and emphasizing their strengths is of central importance when it comes to helping people recover.

Following a Dream

Supporting people's strengths, instilling hope, and boosting self-worth and dignity—these things and more can be found in the story of the person who wanted to be an astronaut. This person dreamed of being an astronaut despite the years he had been ill and consequently out of work. Maybe he dreamed this because of the hero quality of those women and men donning space suits? Maybe it was because he is enamored with space itself, the planets and stars, the rocket ships and moon landings? Whatever his reason, it did not matter because his resource manager would not take him seriously. In fact, when he refused to name another goal, she wrote in her progress report that he was uncooperative and delusional. Needless to say, this professional failed to trigger recovery for this particular individual.

Soon he got another resource manager. But this one also assumed a life in space was nothing but a pipe dream. So the individual went on the same, showing no real progress.

His third resource manager asked the same question, but this time responded, "Let's look into it. Let's find out what one needs to do to become an astronaut." Now the individual had a mission. He went, he found out, he was unbelieving of what it would take to become one! He said, "I don't want to be an astronaut, it is too much work." But his interest in space was real and important to him. It was his dream. So the resource manager worked with him on it. Soon he was working for a company affiliated with NASA, not as an astronaut but in a capacity that allows him to work in the environment that inspires him.

This story is not unique. Many people are told that their dreams are not realistic, yet many people accomplish their dreams despite this lack of support. Imagine what people in recovery could do if the system and the people in the community believed in them. Service providers can help to create a lifelong change by believing in people who have temporarily lost their sense of hope (Orrin, 1998).

As this example demonstrates, a lot of times as human beings, the way we learn is by making our own decisions and mistakes. Critical to recovery is regaining the belief that there are options from which to choose, and this belief is perhaps more important than the options themselves. In order for people to grow in recovery they must be able to make their own choices and decisions as well as take on responsibility for them. The first two mental health professionals were unable to see this person as whole, capable of taking responsibility for himself and his choices. In doing so they undermined his recovery and took away his hopes and dreams. Yet with only a little encouragement and support he was quite able to take control of his life. The potential of the human spirit for healing and renewal should never be underestimated.

> Critical to recovery is regaining the belief that there are options from which to choose, and this belief is perhaps more important than the options themselves.

Recovery: Raising Expectations

Clinicians can begin by looking at every step of the treatment process to see what they can do to instill hope and foster recovery. It is especially impor-

> Recovery is about treating the whole person—identifying their strengths, instilling hope, and helping them to live at an optimal level by teaching them to take responsibility for their life.

tant for clinicians to start and end with a message of hope. For example, just making that first appointment can be a monumental and frightening task. One agency had people write their recovery stories, bound them in a book and put it in the waiting room so that new clients could, from the start, get a message of hope from others. Another agency created a recovery quilt, where people in recovery created a picture of what recovery was for them and this picture was put into each of the squares. This quilt is so beautiful and popular that it now makes the rounds to different government buildings. The quilt project, while projecting positive messages about mental illnesses out into the community, also instilled pride for everyone participating. The demand for the quilt has shown them that their accomplishments in recovery are something other people want to see and know about.

In a society that has for centuries denied hope for people with mental illnesses, things are slowly turning around. The first phases of change brought deinstitutionalization, community support services, and a greater emphasis on rehabilitation and vocational supports. Recovery as a concept, process, and vision is the next phase. Recovery is about treating the whole person—identifying their strengths, instilling hope, and helping them to live at an optimal level by teaching them to take responsibility for their life. It is about the treatment professionals working in partnership with people in recovery. And remembering that recovery is what the individual does; facilitating recovery is what the clinician does; and supporting recovery is what the system and community does.

In the end, clinicians and the system must realize that any and all people, offered the opportunity, accurate knowledge and information, and effective coping mechanisms, recover to the extent that they are able. I started out as a family member. My grandfather spent 40 years in a state mental institution. Back then the sense was "go home and think of him as dead." We did not do that but he still died there. In a sense, when we allow anyone to remain hopeless, we—the system and clinicians—are repeating a similar mistake. Certainly, living in the community is better, but for many being caught up in the system is all that life is about. But the fact is, going to a program every day does not allow the vast majority of people with a serious mental illness to live at their optimal levels. And in a way, encouraging people to stay hopeless is another kind of death—a dying of the heart and soul. Fortunately, the promise of recovery can undo this death. As no person needs to be left behind in the mystery of this journey called life.

References

Anthony, W .A. (1993). Recovery from mental illness: The guiding vision of the mental health service system in the 1990s. *Psychosocial Rehabilitation Journal,* 16(4), 11–23.

Curtis, L. C. (2000). Moving beyond disability: Recovery from psychiatric disorders. One person's perspective. *The Capstone,* 17(2) Summer 2000.

Deegan, P. (1988). Recovery: The lived experience of rehabilitation. *Psychiatric Rehabilitation Journal,* 11(4), 11–19.

Deegan, P. (1996). Recovery as a journey of the heart. *Psychiatric Rehabilitation Journal,* 19(3), 91–97.

Fisher, D. (1996). *Recovery is for everyone.* Video. Lawrence, MA: National Empowerment Center.

Lovejoy, M. (1982). Expectations and the recovery process. *Schizophrenia Bulletin,* 8(4), 605–609.

Orrin, D. (1997). Hope and its important role in recovery. Presentation at the AMI-IAPSRS Michigan Conference "Making Connections: Improving Quality of Life," October 21.

Orrin, D. (1998). A consumer/survivor perspective: The role of hope in the recovery process. *Community Support Network News,* 13(1), Spring. Boston University, Center for Psychiatric Rehabilitation.

Russinova, Z. (1998). Promoting recovery from mental illness Through hope-inspiring strategies. *Community Support Network News,* 13(1), Spring. Boston University, Center for Psychiatric Rehabilitation.

Spaniol, L. & Zipple, A. M. (1997). *Working with families that include a person with a mental illness: Selected readings.* Boston University, Center For Psychiatric Rehabilitation, Boston, MA.

Stocks, M. (1995). In the eye of the beholder. *Psychiatric Rehabilitation Journal,* 19(1), 89–91.

Towson, MD: The Council on Quality and Leadership in Supports for People with Disabilities.

Weingarten, R. (1994). The ongoing process of recovery. *Psychiatry, 57,* 369–375.

I have been
told that I am
a drain on the
nation, a drain on
society, and a
drain on multiple
individuals'
resources.

This drain calls to me because of all the hurtful things people have said to me over the decades about my mental illness. In sum, I have been told that I am a drain on the nation, a drain on society, and a drain on multiple individuals' resources. Over the years, I have come to believe this, which has become a drain on me. Education about mental illness (the effects of trauma) should be able to reach out to the general public, as well as healthcare professionals. Knowledge and understanding can be powerful weapons in combating stigma.

—Catherine Imbasciati, from *Taking Off the Blinders,* 2005

How I Quit Being a "Mental Patient" and Became a Whole Person with a Neuro-Chemical Imbalance: Conceptual and Functional Recovery from a Psychotic Episode

David J. Fekete

I would like to discuss a pilgrimage that psychosis imposed on me. It is a journey that a PACT (Program of Assertive Community Treatment) team could help others with, and that the Peer Specialist in particular could help with. The pilgrimage I refer to is the overwhelming crisis of identity that psychosis brings as one begins to recover. In the following pages, I will analyze my own descent into the "dark night of the soul" of psychosis and confusion, and my return to the bright light of lucidity. Along the way I discuss my growing self-image as a person with a label. First, I need to define my terms.

Definitions: "Identity"

Identity: Who am I? What am I? What was I? What and who have I become? Identity. After the soul-shattering experience of a psychotic episode and the personality distortions that come with it, no issue is more compelling than the question of identity, and this question can be divided into two parts. The first question is "Who am I?", or self concept. The second question is "What am I?" or "What have I become?" This is the issue of symptoms.

I will discuss identity in relation to the life domain of community. Community is always an important life domain. But it requires special attention during the period of recovery. Without sensitivity from mental health providers to the special needs of a person undergoing recovery, the issue of community will be stumbled through by individuals on their own. The intensive support that a PACT team provides can be an invaluable service to persons who are beginning the laborious process of recovering identity.

Psychosis and Identity

My firsthand introduction to neuro-chemical disorders occurred while I was writing my doctoral dissertation at the University of Virginia in 1992. Something happened to me rather suddenly that I didn't understand. I came to think that language and clothing colors were all a code that everybody but me understood. I even tried talking in this code, as best as I understood it. I became afraid to eat because I couldn't understand the color codes that food packaging had on it. I found myself walking at breakneck speed for miles on trivial errands. My sleep was disturbed. While all this was going on I felt that something was terribly wrong with me. I was swimming in confusion, misunderstanding, and fear, but I didn't know what was happening. In a matter of months I had become psychotic and delusional, but I didn't even know that I was psychotic and delusional. I had never been psychotic before in my life, and I had no education in psychology, so I couldn't make sense of what was happening.

This article was published in the *Psychiatric Rehabilitation Journal*, 2004, 28(2), 189–194, and is reprinted with permission.

I was so ignorant of the mental health field that I couldn't help myself, nor could I respond to the help that initially was offered me. At one point I stormed into a medical hospital complaining of a strange physical ailment. I thought that people were doing things to my body in my sleep—even though I barred my bedroom door with a file cabinet. The doctor at the hospital told me that I did not have the physical ailment of which I complained. They then ushered a psychiatrist into my room. At this point I was torn. On one hand, I was relieved to find out that my physical ailment wasn't there. On the other hand, if my strange physical problem wasn't there, then I knew that there must be something really wrong with my mind. The psychiatrist was direct. She said, "You are delusional; you need medication."

> I was a normal person, or even, I flattered myself to think, an exceptional person. How could I be crazy?

Now I was really confused. I had never been "crazy" before. I was a normal person. I had excelled as an undergraduate. I made the Dean's List the junior and senior year of my undergraduate program. I had been admitted to the Urbana College Academic Society. I was the editor of the college newspaper my junior year. I was elected class president my senior year. I was listed in Who's Who in American Colleges and Universities for 1979–1980. My senior year I was the male lead in the college production of "Bye Bye Birdie."

I went on to take a Master's Degree from Harvard University. I was now a doctoral student at the University of Virginia and had passed my doctoral exams. I had ambitious personal interests. I played Bach fugues and Mozart and Beethoven sonatas on the piano for enjoyment. I performed in a classic rock and jazz band. I wrote music and poetry. I was a normal person, or even, I flattered myself to think, an exceptional person. How could I be crazy?

Not having been educated in the nature of neuro-chemical imbalances, a term I prefer to underscore the medical model of "mental illness," all I knew were those ignorant stereotypes from the media. I knew of "crazy" people from seeing movies like "One Flew Over the Cuckoo's Nest." Crazy people were those eerie figures creeping around the corridors of mental hospitals wearing socks on their hands, giggling hysterically, acting like roosters, and only leaving the mental hospital on day passes. This clearly wasn't me, so I couldn't be crazy. And I thought that there were two classes of people: "crazy" people and "normal" people. If I had had a better understanding of mental health, I might have been quicker to realize that people like me could also have a neuro-chemical imbalance.

Ultimately, I found myself in a psychiatric hospital and by now, being admitted to a hospital was a relief. Now, the issue of identity flooded my consciousness, and I fully identified myself as a "crazy person," a "mental patient." All my own prejudices about neuro-chemical imbalances came crashing down on my own mind. I thought that I was less a part of the human race. I was on the other side of the wall between "normal" people and "crazy" people. I had left society and had become a "mental patient." The locked doors of the psych ward separating us from "normal" people became my dominant metaphor. I was a resident of the psych ward in my own self-image wherever I went geographically. Me as "crazy" now replaced every other image I had formed about myself—scholar, musician, poet.

Identity and Community

My functioning identity as "crazy" affected my efforts for community. I needed company. I was afraid to be alone, but I was inhibited from rejoining society by my own self-image. I was afraid of being known by others as a "crazy" person. I was well aware of the stigma that many people carry for "mental patients." In fact, I carried the stigma myself! And had I not isolated myself by my own self-image, I felt assured that other people would isolate me if they found out that I was a "mental patient." I certainly didn't want anyone in the University to know that I was a "mental patient." So I found myself befriending a "low functioning" person who had a neuro-chemical imbalance.

I was "crazy," like him. Since I thought we were more essentially alike, I thought I should spend my time with him, instead of my academic colleagues. I would meet him in a 24-hour deli and read over and over a passage from T.S. Eliot's *Four Quartets* about darkness coming over the soul. It captures how I was feeling:

> I said to my soul, be still, and let the
> dark come upon you...
> As, in a theatre,
> The lights are extinguished, for the
> scene to be changed...
> I said to my soul, be still, and wait
> without hope
> For hope would be hope for the wrong
> thing; wait without love
> For love would be love for the wrong
> thing;...
> Wait without thought, for you are not
> ready for thought:
> So the darkness shall be the light, and
> the stillness the dancing.
> —Four Quartets, "East Coker," ll. 112–117, 123–128

My new friend used to say, "You look troubled, David." We didn't say much, but he was someone to be with. I also hung out with the young couple who worked at Subway. They expected little of me and they stayed by me.

I have been discussing my identity fears with reference to my academic department. But the same fears can occur with reference to any socially significant group such as family, friends, or co-workers. Persons who have been through the devastations of psychosis can isolate themselves because of similar fears about identity—who they are, and what they are. As mental health professionals, we need to be sensitive to fears that devolve from psychosis. With an awareness of these psychodynamics, we can effectively intervene to move a person through identity crisis to self-possession.

The second identity issue is the question "What am I?" or "What have I become?" After my psychotic episode, my personality had altered radically. Formerly, my life had been characterized by a daring boldness. I was assertive; I loved challenges; I had a drive to excel. Now I had become timid, weak, open, and vulnerable. Everything overwhelmed me. Everyone seemed smarter than I, more knowledgeable, more well-read. Everyone intimidated me. Before, no challenge seemed too great. Now everything seemed too difficult for me—I was afraid to attempt almost anything. Before, I had negotiated intricate jazz chords on the bass enthusiastically in front of filled nightclubs. Now I was afraid when a friend asked me to play a simple three-chord rock song with his band. I had lost my former ambition, my will to fight. I hated what I had become because I knew how I used to be, and I couldn't get back there.

My mind had become disorganized. I had been an outstanding student. I remember how it had been writing the first chapter of my dissertation. I had every footnote and allusion on the tip of my mind. I could see the entire chapter's structure in my mind as I wrote. I knew what I was going to say on the last page while I was writing the first few. My thoughts flew way ahead of my fingers on the computer keyboard. Now, on the second chapter, I couldn't think my way through the argument I was trying to make on the page in front of me. My dissertation director complained about this chapter when I turned in the first draft. He said it lacked an overall coherence. Well, so did the mind that wrote it. I found reading nearly impossible. I couldn't concentrate, couldn't sit still, and my mind was racing on a train of pointless random associations. I couldn't form sober judgements on the texts I was trying to read because all the arguments seemed pointless. I thought about the long road I had traveled to get into the PhD program at the University of Virginia and it didn't look like I had what it would take to finish.

In my present debilitated condition I wasn't in a state to make new acquaintances, other than the low achieving friends I had newly met. It wasn't friendship so much that I needed. By friendship, I mean the mutual sharing of life's accomplishments and sorrows. I didn't have life accomplishments and sorrows now. Life itself was the problem. Nor was I in a condition to share those delightful pleasantries that friendship thrives on. I didn't have delightful pleasantries in me now. Either I was surging with passion and spoke in a rapid, pressured mode, or I was sullen and depressed, and felt hopeless about everything. My quick wit was now replaced with a slow mind. Either through medications or depression, it took me awhile to process input and my memory was shot. When I wasn't speaking a mile a minute, I was verbally clumsy and at a loss to respond to remarks. And all the while I was bothered by racing thoughts. Thus, I wasn't in a condition to enjoy what we mean by friendship. Rather, what I needed now was someone merely to stand by me as the foundations of the known universe fell apart within my mind. This, regrettably, doesn't fall into the province of many traditional therapists with their professional, distanced clinical posture. I desperately needed someone's presence to reassure me. My psychiatrist described this state as being needy, and she pointed out, somewhat uncharitably, that appearing needy is the surest way to scare people away. Yes, I was very needy during this period of recovery.

My overall mood was depressed. Everything had lost its significance for me. Everything seemed meaningless. There was no enjoyment in things that used to amuse me. Even those simple piano pieces I was able to play with my slow mind gave me no reward. There seemed no point in doing anything. I was operating with an extremely low self-image. I saw myself as old, physically deteriorated and, basically, done with life. I seemed to myself to have succeeded at nothing.

At this point I would like to digress briefly in order to contrast the disappointing care I was receiving from older, traditional models with a new approach to mental health care called PACT (Program of Assertive Community Treatment). I have firsthand experience with both models. As a patient, I received care from traditional models in 1992, the year of my first episode. Then, as a Peer Specialist, I participated in the exciting new PACT model when I was hired full time onto a PACT team in 2000—a position I hold to this day.

While I was receiving services from traditional models, my psychiatrist very much gave me the feeling that I was her "mental patient" and she was my doctor. I didn't get the feeling that I was a whole person talking to another whole person. My self-image would have been greatly improved if my doctor had

The whole structure of traditional mental health services reinforces that depersonalization of the doctor/patient relationship.

adopted Ralph Waldo Emerson's posture of "a man speaking to men." My new identity was forming during the period when I saw my doctor every other week. She was my sole link to an understanding of my condition. And her unspoken perceptions of me, and the way she related to me contributed to my developing self-image. Her clinical posture deprived me of a feeling of full personhood and reinforced the doctrine that I was her "mental patient."

The whole structure of traditional mental health services reinforces that depersonalization of the doctor/patient relationship. Traditional mental health services center around the doctor's office. I would go to the doctor's office for a one-hour session every other week. There, I sat in a chair about ten feet from the psychiatrist's chair and talked about issues in my life outside the office. I went to the hospital pharmacy to pick up my medicine. My life centered around the clinic. The clinic defined my life, and so my identity. I was thus defined as a patient, a "mental patient."

By contrast, the PACT model affirms the whole person by a number of methods. When I was hired as a Peer Specialist, I was able to witness the difference in modes of care between the PACT model and traditional services that I received when I was a patient. I found that the differing models of care provide differing implications for client identity formation. While the posture of traditional services is doctor to patient, the posture of PACT is side by side. Rather than sitting in a chair talking about my life outside the clinic, the PACT model locates care in the actual community where life issues occur. While one might characterize traditional methods of care as theorizing about life outside the clinic, one would characterize PACT methods as training in life settings. Thus the actual life of the persons we serve is the center of care, not the clinic. The message conveyed by the PACT model is that the life of the persons we serve is what matters. As members of the PACT team, we deliver medicine to the person we serve in his or her home. We go out for coffee with the person we serve. We go shopping with the people we serve. We cook with them. We apartment hunt with them—side by side.

And the PACT model recognizes the need for rehabilitation in the area of community. It calls for a "Social Development and Functioning" assessment when the new person is admitted for services. During this assessment, my own problems with friendships and community would have come up as a problem area in need of care, had PACT been available to me. I don't even know if my psychiatrist even thought about the deep social problems my search for an identity was causing. The PACT model also insists that time be spent in the area of socialization with persons being served. The Pact Manual states that the PACT team organize "individual and group social and recreational activities to structure a client's time, increase social experiences, and provide opportunities to practice social skills and receive feedback and support" (Allness & Knoedler, 1998: 62).

Here is one place where the Peer Specialist can be uniquely useful. The Peer Specialist is a recognized member of the treatment team that also shares the whole depth of experience that the client is undergoing. The Peer Specialist has a special understanding of the drives that cause isolation after the disorientation of psychosis. As "one who has been there," the Peer Specialist can foster a solidarity with the person being served. With this special bond of mutual understanding, the Peer Specialist recognizes the disorientation that can occur during recovery and stays in the moment with the person being served, waiting in the darkness, speaking through the turmoil. The Peer Specialist can thus supply needs for community that go beyond ordinary friendship, until the person being served passes through the recovery period and is ready again to strike up those endearments that so enrich our lives. Here, mutual camaraderie becomes a therapeutic tool.

But when I was recovering from my first episode in 1992, I didn't have the benefit of a PACT team to guide my rehabilitation. The traditional services I received helped me realize that I needed medicine, and they provided medicine management. The medicine I received did nothing short of a miracle for my delusions, and over a period of time a great deal of my functioning returned.

I still had the issue of identity to deal with. One of the early concepts that liberated me from the metaphor of the mental hospital was the medical model for my condition. By now I knew that I had something called bipolar disorder, but my psychiatrist didn't tell me anything about the illness. As I grew to understand the medical model of bipolar disorder, I was able to overcome the stigma associated with my illness and to redefine my person as it relates to my illness. I found out that the chemicals that shoot forth from my neuro-transmitters are imbalanced. This means that my illness isn't mental at all—it is physical. It is like a broken arm. I am not mentally ill. My illness is not some scary mental thing. It is a physical thing, like every other normal, non-scary physical illness. I am an ordinary person with a physical disorder of the same type as diabetes, or appendicitis, or the flu. This changes the way I see myself, when I understand that I have a bodily illness instead of a mental illness. Conceptually, it removes me from the "funny farm" and puts me in an ordinary hospital.

> There is me, and then there is my illness....I am not defined by my illness.

And as a physical illness, I distinguish between bipolar disorder and what I mean by me, or my identity. My illness is a separate, alien thing from my identity. There is me, and then there is my illness. I am a whole, functioning person with defective neuro-transmitters. I am not defined by my illness. This means that I am not a different class of person. I am not an illness. I am not a "mental patient." I am a person of the same kind as others, with a specific physical disorder. I am back with the regular, "normal" human race.

The walls of the psych ward crumbled further in my mind as I came to see that others with my illness had contributed to society. I found out that my two favorite writers, Hemingway and T. S. Eliot, each had a neuro-chemical disorder. In fact, T. S. Eliot wrote his great epic The Waste Land while he was in a Swiss sanitarium. The significance of this fact can hardly be overestimated. First of all, it made having a neuro-chemical imbalance OK because these men were pre-eminently OK. But secondly, and more importantly, these great writers not only lived in society, but they had a hand in shaping the society in which they lived. Our western culture is a product of the efforts of individuals with a neuro-chemical imbalance. I am a part of my society, and it is a part of me. I was now able to embrace my world again, as I had before my episode.

Ernest Hemingway and T. S. Eliot gave me another insight into what it means to have a neuro-chemical imbalance. If these men could live the lives they did, and contribute and create as they did, and still be, technically, what people call crazy, then crazy comes to mean something very different from what we commonly think of as crazy. Ultimately, I was able to completely discard the word "crazy" as something that has no basis in reality. "Crazy" means something unexpected, weird, mysterious. Hollywood depicts crazy people as collections of random, silly behavior. But the behaviors of bipolar disorder are not random. In fact, they are so predictable they can be listed specifically in a book no less hallowed than the DSM-IV. The Hollywood meaning of "crazy," which unfortunately is largely the common meaning of "crazy," simply does not exist. I am not "crazy" because the meaning of that word does not exist.

Understanding the medical model made acceptance of bipolar disorder more acceptable for me. I think the reason why there is so much denial among persons with a neuro-chemical imbalance is because they are misinformed about what they have to accept. I can accept the concept that I am a whole person with a neuro-chemical imbalance (although I might not be happy about discovering that I have a disability). But I, and any other person, will vehemently reject the label of being "crazy." Rightly so. If persons are not clear about the physical cause of their disability, then fear, stigma, and misunderstanding will be their only options for identity formation. These identity options would, and should, be denied by anyone. I long for the day when the medical model becomes the dominant paradigm for neuro-chemical imbalances in culture. That will make acceptance much easier and eliminate the damaging stigmas that persist today. Until that day comes, it is imperative for mental health professionals to think and work from the medical model, and above all to see the person, not the illness. We all can play a part in making acceptance acceptable.

As a Peer Specialist, I have been privileged to witness a client erupt in surprise, relief, and joy when I told him, "You're not mentally ill!" With that one statement I shattered years of internalized stigma. But I was emphatic about the fact that he and I require medicine to make our brain chemicals work right. And as a Peer Specialist, I was in a position to establish a tighter partnership with the client than may be possible for other mental health workers. I said, "You have what I have." With that statement the "us and them" perception that can arise between a client and a mental health practitioner was eliminated. The client was much more willing to listen to what I had to say about the medical model when I was using the word "we." "We have neurons that don't work right without medicine." Using the inclusive "we," the Peer Specialist dissolves the isolation that so many persons with a neuro-chemical imbalance feel, and a healthy solidarity is fostered. As a functioning professional, the Peer Specialist is living testimony to the achievement possible with faithful adherence to a medical regimen.

When a client understands that he or she has a physical disability, not a mental illness, then medicine compliance is more reasonable. It makes perfect sense to take medicine to fix your body. No such close logical relation exists between the nebulous mind and medicine.

Seeing myself as a whole person with a physical disorder has made my reintegration into society much easier. I now see myself as just as much a part of society as I was before my episode. My fear of others and what they might think is gone—although it is still startling to notice the reaction that erupts in others when I tell them that I have bipolar disorder, even among people who have known me for a while, and, I regret to say, even among mental health professionals. Sometimes the blanket term "mentally ill" covers all my other attributes—a Harvard graduate with a PhD from the University of Virginia, a scholar, a teacher, a musician, a writer, a mental health worker, or other aspects of my functioning character.

I am happy to say that many of my symptoms have abated. For this I credit the medical community and especially the influence of Zyprexa. In fact, after I had been on lithium for about 9 months, my dissertation director told me that the chapters I turned in were the best writing he had ever seen from me. When it came time to defend my dissertation orally, I was able to listen patiently to the often-strident criticisms of my work, and to respond calmly and methodically to my questioners. Lithium had given me the capacity to hold back and not respond with a knee jerk to every stimulus. So while I may have lost my quick wit, I had gained patience and clarity of thought.

> I have personal relationships now. I have good friends. I have a good life.

I'm not sure that I have returned to the same person I was before my episode. This can be one of the most difficult aspects about recovery. We may not exactly "recover." We may become someone different from what we were. Although listening to music still carries me into raptures of delight, I have questions about my ability to perform. My mind still works a little slow, so it's not as easy for me to find the right note when the beat demands me to be there. However, I am taking bass guitar lessons to see if I can recover some of the joy that music used to bring me. Some days I feel the kick I used to; many days, though, the thrill isn't there. I don't know what to attribute this musical instability to–lingering depression, medicine, or simply older age. I sleep more than I used to. I don't know what returning to school would be like, as I don't trust my memory as I used to.

But I like who I am now. I finished my doctoral program and received my PhD in 1994. I still love to write. I write poetry. I completed a book about love and spirituality that was published in October of 2003. I also have completed a scholarly article about a medieval romance, which was published in January 2004. I have been a college teacher for 8 years and have loved every bit of it. Now I work full time on a PACT team as a Peer Specialist. I find it rewarding to work with my peers as they grow and prosper according to the capacity each has. It is a privilege to be able to share the insights I have found in my own recovery with others and to learn from them. I have personal relationships now. I have good friends. I have a good life. Having a neuro-chemical imbalance is not the end of life as we knew it. There is a vast spectrum of ways to live and love life with a neuro-chemical imbalance. To borrow Winston Churchill's words, another great person with a neuro-chemical imbalance, never give up. Never give up. Never, never give up.

Postscript to original article: I have followed up my university education with divinity training, returning to my original career calling. I am now employed full time as an ordained Protestant minister. I take my pills every morning and night, and never think about bipolar disorder any more. That is recovery.

Sincerely,
Rev. Dr. David J. Fekete

References

Allness, D. J. & Knoedler, W. H. (1998). *The PACT model of community based treatment for persons with severe and persistent mental illnesses.* Arlington, Virginia: NAMI Anti Stigma Foundation.

Eliot, T. S. (1971). *Four quartets.* New York: Harcourt Brace & Company.

People close
the door before
getting to know
the true "inside"
of me.

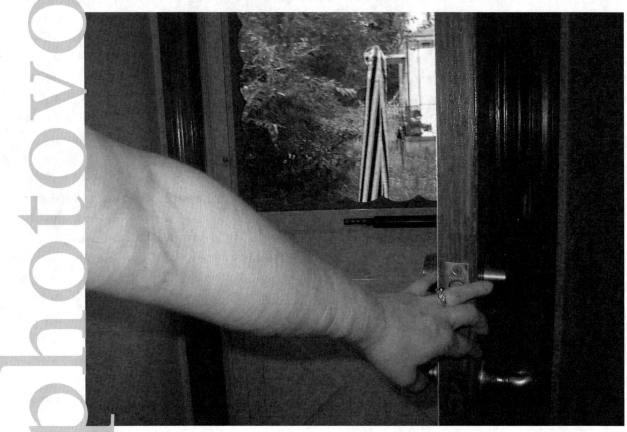

Often I am stigmatized because of the scars on my arms. People close the door before getting to know the true "inside" of me. Sometimes I feel the causes of the battle scars were easier to recover from than the cruelty from everyday people and the health care professionals judging me. They make an assumption that I am dangerous or scary without ever getting to know me. There are reasons I have these scars. It would be a perfect world if people did not judge one another because of someone being different, just because they did not have an understanding of the issue. Educating the everyday public and health care providers on why and how things like this happen will lessen the stigma. Understanding something usually takes away most of the mystery—people are not as afraid.

—Karen, from *Picturing My Health,* 2005

First Psychosis Prodrome: Rehabilitation and Recovery

Ian Chovil

Early intervention in first psychosis programs were once just research projects but are increasingly a part of the continuum of mental health services in Australia, Britain, Canada, and Norway. It is a very logical development in the treatment of psychotic disorders. The Canadian National CMHA has created a document, "Early Psychosis Intervention, A Framework for Strategic Planning," which outlines the rationale and components of this intervention (Ehman, Gilbert & Hansen, 2004).

There are measurable gains to be made in reducing the duration of untreated psychosis (DUP) to less than 6 months from the 2 years that is prevalent now. There are some conflicting reports about this, but well controlled studies such as Malla et al. (2002) report significant gains. It is preferable to engage someone with a psychotic disorder in a therapeutic partnership at the first psychosis, instead of later in that individual's life when the process may be much more problematic. Treatment per se will have a limited value without a therapeutic partnership as described by Hamilton-Wilson and Hobbs (Hamilton-Wilson & Hobbs, 1995).

As a consumer, my interest is the loss of functioning experienced during the prodrome. I had an insidious onset of schizophrenia beginning in high school and gradually lost my human relationships over a 9-year period without anyone realizing I was ill. I was completely alone by the time I was homeless in Calgary for 6 months in 1980. I remained in psychosis and untreated for the next 10 years. Eventually I got in trouble with the law, and was court ordered to see a psychiatrist as a condition of my probation. That led to a hospitalization for alcoholism and the beginning of treatment for schizophrenia upon discharge in 1990. I've experienced 14 years of very gradual recovery on medication since then, and now work half time at a psychiatric hospital as a consumer consultant. In my employment I am meeting with a variety of first psychosis patients as they are being discharged from the Intensive Care Unit at the hospital to share my experiences. I'm also making 45 presentations a year on mental illness and schizophrenia to high school classes, usually grade 11 health classes. I keep remembering my experience of illness at their age, 16, a pivotal year for me.

There is surprisingly little research of first psychosis prodrome, probably because it is usually observable only through retrospective enquiry. Yung and McGorry published several papers based on the data developed through the Australian early intervention program (McGorry et al., 1995; Yung & McGorry, 1996a; Yung & McGorry, 1996b). Researchers generally have been looking for predictive symptoms of schizophrenia and psychosis, not at rehabilitation issues arising from a prolonged prodrome experience (e.g., McGorry et al., 1995). At best, the impact of the prodrome is described as "premorbid functioning" in first psychosis literature (eg. Malla et al., 2002). The term *prodrome* also is used to describe the decompensation prior to a relapse which can be confusing.

This article was published in the *Psychiatric Rehabilitation Journal*, 2005, 28(4), 407–410, and is reprinted with permission.

Møller and Husby completed a thorough review of psychiatric papers on first psychosis prodrome pointing out inconsistencies in concepts, defining symptoms, language, and statistical terms, all of which results in a lack of consensus in the literature on the prodrome (Møller and Husby, 2000). Their particular perspective was actually the most congruent with my prodrome experience in my limited review of the literature.

> It is preferable to engage someone with a psychotic disorder in a therapeutic partnership at the first psychosis, instead of later in that individual's life when the process may be much more problematic.

As a consumer, the most important feature of the first psychosis prodrome is in many ways most readably identified by retrospective enquiry: the loss of functioning the individual experiences. They become very isolated socially. They fail and drop out of school. They struggle to remain employed in any paid capacity. They may become preoccupied by religion and mysticism. They have increasing levels of anxiety each year of disability and may have trouble sleeping. They start smoking marijuana daily, and drinking to excess.

The individual becomes unable to function in the highly competitive world of late adolescence and early adulthood, when career and romance choices are being evaluated and chosen, when one's place in the world is being defined. Although physicians are unable to establish a diagnosis, the parents and immediate family often are only too aware that something is really wrong with their son or daughter during the prodrome. They just don't know what. I personally would have been hard pressed to describe what I was experiencing during my prodrome. I did realize something was wrong. My best guess was something psychological, or even sociological, rather than medical. I never would have seen my family physician about my adjustment problems.

Cohen et al. reported an average 4 years prodrome before 2 years of DUP for males in Toronto and 8 years prodrome before 2 years of DUP in females (Cohen, Gotowiec & Seeman, 2000). Most studies agree the prodrome is about twice as long as the DUP, but the actual lengths of time seem to vary considerably amongst different studies for probably a variety of reasons. There are significant differences depending on whether the figure is reported as the mean, the median, or the average. There are differences of opinion in what symptoms signify the beginning of illness. The total duration of illness (DUI) prior to treatment can be 5 to 10 years, and is occurring at a key developmental period during the transition from dependent adolescent to independent adult.

In my prodrome, I seemed to lose functioning in social realms long before I started to lose academic ability. Cornblatt spends some time discussing the progression of symptoms of high risk individuals in the New York High Risk Project and the Hillside Recognition and Prevention Program in her paper (Cornblatt, 2002). Not all types of schizophrenia are necessarily included in a study of high risk individuals where one or more parents have schizophrenia, but such studies do not face the limitations faced by retrospective enquiry. Essentially, the individual typically has had difficulty with attention from a very early age. In early adolescence, they lose social skills and social competence, and later they have academic losses and employment losses until they experience psychosis.

The movie "A Beautiful Mind" captured this progression very well, the movie opening with Nash in his prodrome experiencing a significant loss of his social skills and social competence; something many viewers might decide was his natural personality, rather than the untreated disease process he was experiencing.

I can't actually establish the loss of social functioning in my prodrome. It seems to almost precede adolescence. I had increasing levels of social anxiety, difficulty relating with people, difficulty developing romantic relationships, difficulty with authority; all accompanied by very low self esteem and lack of self-confidence. That could describe many teenagers.

I can establish clearly what I would call my "academic prodrome," as beginning in grade 12 at age 17. In grade 11, I scored in the top three percentile in the provincial math contest written by every grade 10 and 11 high school student in Ontario. In grade 12 my interest in school dropped, my ability to do the actual work declined considerably, my ability to even focus on the required work just disappeared. I lost any interest in competitive sports. I remember having a very low threshold for stress of any sort. I dropped all my male friendships. My mother says I seemed to lose my ambition at age 18.

I probably would have failed high school, but I had enrolled in an experimental program that didn't stress grades. My interests switched during grade 12 from math and physics to English and psychology. My one and only girlfriend had strong interests in English, history and, especially, feminism. Those became my interests. I also read about the Human Potential movement, about Gestalt therapy, R. D. Laing, and Rolfing, because that was what I thought was most relevant to my problems. I knew I needed help of some sort because I was losing my capability to participate in life.

My girlfriend eventually left me, which was a very painful experience, because I had become quite dependent on her. Somehow I was admitted to university, although I didn't have any career plans of any sort. I struggled to adapt to university and began to believe I was a genius. I was in emotional turmoil, struggling with human relationships, averse to any competitive challenge, but quick to criticize established authority. I also became increasingly preoccupied with shamanism, witchcraft, alchemy, and the Kabala, a symptom noted by Møller and Husby (Møller & Husby, 2000). There is no competitive struggle in mysticism, no career development, no potential financial compensation of any sort. I was drinking heavily at parties, and smoking more and more marijuana each year at university.

Eventually my only friends (and I use the term loosely), were a few male marijuana smoking buddies, and smoking marijuana was virtually the only activity we engaged in. I was smoking daily in an effort to drop out of the competitive struggles of university life. I was identifying strongly with the Rastafarians and their sacred herb.

I almost dropped out of university every year I attended. In two Early Intervention programs in Ottawa and London, 50% and 40%, respectively, of the clients are smoking marijuana frequently enough to interfere with their recovery on medication (Claudia Hampel, 2003, personal communication) (Rahul Manchanda, 2003, personal communication).

By graduate school at age 25, I had stopped smoking marijuana. I was becoming extremely anxious about employment because I didn't

> The individual has typically had difficulty with attention from a very early age. In early adolescence they lose social skills and social competence, and later they have academic losses and employment losses....

have any actual career experience of any sort. I also was sliding into psychosis with very clear episodes of reality distortion, and I was kicked out of school that year. Within a year I was homeless.

The increasing anxiety caused by the loss of functioning ability is probably a significant factor in the emergence of psychosis. Where financial resources allow, patients may avoid that growing anxiety by simply hiding out in their parent's basement. That anxiety also may interfere with adequate treatment, since the medication per se doesn't directly address the issues causing the anxiety, like unemployment, and lost friendships.

People in prodrome will have developed various adaptations to being forced out of competitive environments and to their inability to even associate with their peers. They probably will not only have dropped out of competitive development processes, such as career acquisition; they may have devalued that activity so that it is no longer desirable to them. People tend to drop out of activities they can't do. In treatment, people who have adapted to the prodrome may be very inclined to resume smoking marijuana, to resume their previous relationship with the world, as established during their prodrome. They will tend to engage in a reality construction based on their prodrome experience.

> To simply treat the presenting psychosis is inadequate. It is essential that rehabilitation resources be developed to maximize the potential recovery.

These first psychosis patients may not have planned the course to a successful career. They may have no long term romantic aspirations of any sort. A significant number of the males will have few non-marijuana smoking friends, and very weak membership in any non-marijuana smoking peer group. Some will be complete loners. Some will be outcasts and rebels. They may be very reluctant to return to school, even if they haven't finished high school. The delay of even a single year could brand them as a "loser" in a competitive environment like high school.

I might have been able to predict that John Nash would write his PhD thesis on noncompetitive game theory. I was very averse to any competitive struggle, to capitalism in general, hence my identification with Rastafarianism. In university, my marijuana friends created a New Athlektic Front, an organization dedicated to noncompetitive sports. We demanded funding equal to that received by the university teams, like football, skiing, hockey, etc., which were traveling to compete with other university teams.

To us, those teams were symbolic of the "Neofascist Sports Complex"; a concept I still think has merit. When you only have winners and losers, people in prodrome are very likely to be losers. If you're competent in a competitive world, you don't notice how competitive it really is. Success is expected and just comes naturally.

First psychosis patients not in an early intervention program are now generally stabilized on medication and receive minimal follow-up because the best response to medication is during the first psychosis (Brian Furlong 2004, personal communication). The psychosis itself is probably the easiest symptom to treat. Treating the prodromal symptoms is a different story altogether, and relapse rates will depend on how well those symptoms are addressed. Typically they aren't. There are many other people who are much sicker, with very well documented treatment histories, and they are generally a much higher priority for rehabilitation services because they have to be able to live successfully in the community. Many first psychosis patients simply return to live with their parents. Family education through a multifamily education program is generally not a standard practice, and so even the families who are facing a very steep learning curve, receive minimal support. This is not a recipe for successful treatment of schizophrenia.

With my disability I've learned that you are faced with creating a comfortable niche in a highly competitive world. You have to adapt to your illness, and you have to adapt to the world around you. People recovering from a first psychosis probably have the potential to experience a significant recovery from the disability they experienced during their prodrome.

People with DUPs of less than 6 months are likely to experience full remission of psychotic symptoms, although Malla et al. found that negative symptoms are by nature less responsive to medication (Malla et al., 2002). I couldn't find any research that looked at cognitive symptoms. I couldn't find any research that looked at recovery from a first psychosis in what to me, as a consumer, is the fundamental parameter of the prodrome, functioning ability.

I did find research where the relapse rate for first episode schizophrenia is 50% in the first year of remission (Wiersma, Nienhuis, Sloeff & Giel, 1998). At a minimum, we need to prevent these first psychosis patients from further deterioration in functioning resulting from multiple relapses. The gains made reducing the DUP to less than 6 months in early intervention programs will be lost without effective relapse prevention.

We are going to have to recognize that the prodrome experience will have a profound impact on relapse rates, on rehabilitation success, and on recovery in every sense of the word; and develop resources accordingly. To simply treat the presenting psychosis is inadequate. It is essential that rehabilitation resources be developed to maximize the potential recovery and relapse prevention in a population that has been adapting to an undiagnosed illness many years prior to treatment, during the critical developmental transition from dependent adolescent to independent adult. The prodrome is presently an uncharted period of disability during adolescence that is likely to have a profound effect on an individual's future expectations and successes in treatment.

> You have to adapt to your illness, and you have to adapt to the world around you.

References

Cohen, R., Gotowiec, A. & Seeman, M. (2000). Duration of pretreatment phases in schizophrenia: Women and men. *Canadian Journal of Psychiatry, 45*, 544–548.

Cornblatt, B. (2002). The New York High Risk Project to the Hillside Recognition and Prevention (RAP) Program. *American Journal of Medical Genetics, 114*, 956–966.

Ehman, T., Gilbert, M., & Hanson, L. (2004). *Early psychosis intervention, a framework for strategic planning.* Canadian Mental Health Association http://www.cmha.ca/english/intrvent/images/EPI_Policy_ENG.pdf.

Furlong, B. (2004) Medical Director, Trillium Intensive Care Unit, Community Division, Homewood Health Centre, Guelph.

Hamilton Wilson, J., & Hobbs, H. (1995). Therapeutic partnership: A model for clinical practice. *Journal of Psychosocial Nursing and Mental Health Services, 33*(2), 27–30.

Hampel, C. (2003). Program manager, Ottawa First Episode Psychosis Clinic.

Malla, A., Norman, R., Manchanda, R., Ahmed, M., Scholten, D., Harricaran, R., Cortese, L., & Takhar, J. (2002) One year outcome in first episode psychosis: Influence of DUP and other predictors. *Schizophrenia Research, 54*, 231–242.

Manchanda, R. (2003). Program Director, Prevention and Early Intervention Program.

McGorry, P., McFarlane, C., Patton, G., Bell, R., Hibbert, M., Jackson, H., & Bowes, G. (1995). The prevalence of prodromal features of schizophrenia in adolescence: A preliminary survey. *Acta Psychiatrica Scandinavica, 92*, 241–249.

Møller, P., & Husby, R. (2000). The initial prodrome in schizophrenia: Searching for naturalistic core dimensions of experience and behaviour. *Schizophrenia Bulletin, 26*(1), 217–232.

Wiersma, D., Nienhuis, F., Sloeff, C. J, & Giel, R. (1998). Natural course of schizophrenic disorders: A 15-year follow-up of a Dutch incidence cohort. *Schizophrenic Bulletin, 24*(1), 75–85.

Yung, A., & McGorry, P. (1996a). The initial prodrome in psychosis: Descriptive and qualitative aspects. *Australian and New Zealand Journal of Psychiatry, 30*, 587–599.

Yung, A., & McGorry, P. (1996b). The prodromal phase of first episode psychosis: Past and current conceptualizations. *Schizophrenia Bulletin, 22*(2), 353–370.

We have to knock
down the prison
walls. Education is
our bulldozer.

photovoice

These flowers are me. I am something bright and intelligent with a sweet essence of soothing compassion. But I cannot share these qualities because I am behind a prison wall called stigma. I am not free to bloom and show the world my beauty that has been taken from me through society's fear and ignorance. Fortunately, that can change. Society is composed of individuals, and individuals can be re-educated. We have to knock down the prison walls. Education is our bulldozer.

—Catherine Imbasciati, from *Taking Off the Blinders,* 2005

Recovery Commentary: With the Passage of Time

William Stride

Imagine that one night the phone rings during dinner, and the caller informs you that your son is being held in a state mental hospital 3,000 miles away. Panicked, you immediately make arrangements to go to the aid of your son. Three days later, you are climbing the steps to the door of a locked psychiatric ward, and a mental health worker lets you in. As you step inside, it is like entering some strange foreign city for the first time. What you see is shocking: thick clouds of cigarette smoke fill the room, freakish people and your semi-catatonic son sitting at the opposite end of the room. "What happened to my son?" you ask the doctor. What has happened to him is that he suffered a schizophrenic break; an affliction not so well understood and which in the beginning has no clear prognosis or outlook for the future.

The parents meet with a team of doctors almost every day. They are fed explanations of the different theories of schizophrenia. They are told about all of the different medications, their strengths, weaknesses and side effects. They are told of different therapies and given statistical breakdowns as to the likelihood of partial, full, or no recovery at all. In learning these things a hazy and uncertain future begins to materialize on the horizon.

The person undergoing the break tells a different story. Although the onset of a psychotic break can brew beneath the surface for quite some time, the break itself can be quite sudden. The break is obvious to observers, yet somehow remains hidden from the person. This phenomenon is further compounded if the person is immediately hospitalized. Suddenly the person becomes a client and is thrust into a strange new environment full of people they are scared of and repulsed by. As a client, the person is forced to take drugs, is held in the quiet room, sometimes in restraints, constantly being interviewed by doctors and psychologists, and lastly, he is told over and over that he has a serious mental illness.

When this radical change of external circumstances comes simultaneously with the break, it can be very hard for a person to see the change in their own behavior. He or she may blame all of their problems on the simple fact that they are being held in a mental hospital against their will. Anyone else in this position probably would think the same.

The third party in this drama consists of the mental health professionals who are often new to the field. These mental health professionals are resident psychiatrists, psychologists-in-training, newly hired social workers, nurses, and mental health workers. All three parties, client, family, and new hires in the mental health system, have one thing in common: They are blind as to what comes with the passage of time. They only see the present condition of the client and have no knowledge as to what can possibly happen in one month, one year, or ten years. The only way they can know what will change for the person is to follow the progress of the client over these spans of time. When a resident psychiatrist begins working in a state hospital ward, he/she soon realizes that what was learned in studying books does not provide ade-

This article was published in the *Psychiatric Rehabilitation Journal*, 2006, 29(3), 226–228, and is reprinted with permission.

quate preparation for the challenges that must be faced in caring for clients. The resident psychiatrist often puts on the face of the objective, stoical, clinical observer because that is what was emphasized and learned in school. As time goes by, the resident's human feelings will begin to surface, and he or she may mourn the losses that the client experiences and rejoice at individual successes. If at this point the resident psychiatrist tries to push down personal feelings and attempt to forget them, he or she will never be a very good psychiatrist. Where the sphere of ideas intersects with the world of emotions, good work can be done. Empathy and compassion are for talking to those who are feeling pain and sorrow. In order to talk to the pain, one must allow oneself to feel the pain and then something can be done.

> Where the sphere of ideas intersects with the world of emotions, good work can be done.

At this point, the person diagnosed with a mental illness, their family, and caregivers set off on a lifelong journey down the road called "recovery." Recovery is not an end result or destination, as many people like to think of it. Recovery is a process, a way of living and caring for oneself. It means creating a new lifestyle, changing one's world view as a client in ways that counterbalance the illness. Successful recovery means less and less interference from the illness and the desired result: more freedom.

When a son or daughter becomes ill, a great deal of responsibility is put on the shoulders of their parents. The parents, not knowing what to do, usually revert to the only role they have available: they treat their son or daughter like an adolescent. Unfortunately when this happens, their son or daughter very quickly learns how to act like an adolescent. It does not work well when parents treat delusion as some kind of eccentricity or depression as some kind of sudden laziness.

A homeless man once said to me: "Reality is how you perceive it." No statement could better sum up the application of therapy. Where one cannot change the world around them, there is the option of changing their perception of it. People, places, and events that upset the client can be made less ominous, not by removing them from a client's life but by changing a client's relation to them.

A client can learn that it is OK to take time off from school in order to deal with other adverse circumstances. Likewise, a client also can learn that it is alright to take an extra year or two to finish a degree and that advisors, employers, and mentors actually may have a great deal of patience and understanding when it comes to a client's situation. It is also helpful to learn that not everyone will be accepting of an illness, but there are many people who will be, and it is those people that a client must seek out and incorporate into the foundation of their recovery.

In the early days of dealing with the illness, a client may decompensate and not know what is happening or how to cope with it. Things can get out of control quickly and for a person new to recovery, they often can end up in the hospital again. This is normal. Over time, a person's perception of their internal warning signs takes on more sophistication, and they are more able to keep close tabs on their mental, emotional, and physical states. When this process is a success, a client will end up in the hospital less and less often.

There also will come a time in a client's recovery when a major milestone is reached; no more hospitalizations. When that milestone occurs, neither the client nor anyone else is aware of it. The discharge is like any other discharge. However, over time a client will decompensate and make visits to the emergency room. Perhaps, the person is interviewed, and to his or her surprise, he or she is not admitted to the hospital. Over time, there are more trips to the emergency room, but the person is not admitted. Finally the trips to the emergency room stop all together, and everyone involved with

> Recovery is a process, a way of living and caring for oneself.

the person's treatment suddenly sits up and takes notice. The guardianships are dropped; the person is granted independent housing and receives many other new freedoms. Once again the client has become a person and takes great pride in the fact that he or she has escaped the revolving door of hospitalization. He or she has attained a new station in life: self-reliance.

> Successful reintegration requires that a person's life and work be in alignment with his or her dreams and talents. This is the only way a person can grow and feel fulfilled.

Staying out of the hospital for one year is very significant as one year contains all of the seasonal highs and lows; all of the holidays; all anniversaries of births, deaths, marriages, divorces and first hospitalization. If a client historically has been going to the hospital two or three times a year and then goes for a whole year without being admitted, it is a clue that a real right turn has taken place. If a client can stay out of the hospital for a year, he or she could certainly stay out for two or three years, or even for the rest of his or her life.

People who have been struck with mental illness, especially in the young adult group (18–30 years of age), are ambitious people who may have lofty goals and big plans for their future. They were engaged in or preparing for medical school, law school, graduate school, or high powered careers, or were struck with the illness halfway through their undergraduate career. At the onset of the illness, continuing with these plans usually becomes impossible. Later in recovery the question comes up: can these lofty goals now be pursued?

It is interesting to note that on the state hospital admissions wards the most irate, angry, and bitter clients are the high functioning members of the young adult group. They have been removed forcibly from the life they had and committed to the state institution. Their energy and passion allow them to reject the diagnosis and stay in denial for long periods of time. When the pendulum swings in the other direction, their resolve and perseverance allows them the possibility of doing quite well in recovery.

Over time the perception of going back to school or re-entering their career surely will change. These endeavors become symbolic of a life once lived, a better life, an escape from the system. The person becomes like the ghetto athlete shooting for fame and fortune on the pro basketball courts. Or like a smart, hardworking, and yet impoverished high school student trying to earn a scholarship to a good university. His or her aim is singular: to get to a better place, a new station in life, the station of dignity and respect, freedom and independence.

Over a long period of time something like graduate school may have become like putting a square peg in a round hole. A person may want to do something along these lines, but in reality, he or she may not be happy doing it. Enter: *Love's Executioner.* Maybe they want to study some new subject or try some kind of work that they have never done before.

In summary, successful reintegration requires that a person's life and work be in alignment with his or her dreams and talents. This is the only way a person can grow and feel fulfilled. Some of the projects that the client wants to

> If something does not work, don't lose hope, try again later.

launch may have his or her caregivers taking a deep breath, but it is the client's right to do these things. If something does not work, don't lose hope, try again later.

He has a zest for
life, a love of
people, and
seldom complains
although often in
pain. He's pretty
remarkable.

This is my Uncle John. He is 88 years old, served in
two wars, and is currently retired. Uncle John also has
battled cancer, several strokes, and has rheumatoid
arthritis. He takes a walk every morning, takes care of
his apartment, cooks his own meals, and is extremely
popular in the complex where he lives. I have an
appreciation of wellness through Uncle John. He has
a zest for life, a love of people, and seldom complains
although often in pain. He's pretty remarkable.

—Gloria, from *Wellness As I See It*, 2003

CHAPTER 3

Managing Life's Stresses

Marriage and Mental Illness

Valerie Fox

I have not read anything regarding persons who marry while living with serious, persistent mental illness. I married in the 1960s when persistent mental illness was considered a "nervous breakdown" and not an ongoing disease. With this article, I want to educate and explore thought in other persons who might share the same problems I experienced. I want to give a voice to the isolation I felt while married, coping with my illness. I felt so different from other married women with my closeted illness. I have two beautiful daughters who suffered a tragedy in their young lives when I became ill, yet our love seems to have survived and our relationship each day grows. With this article I want to give a voice to one marriage and mental illness. I want someone who reads this to say, "Yes, I feel like that; I know I'm not alone."

I think it is important to start this account by saying I grew up in a one-parent home with an "Auntie Mame" type mother, loving and very individualistic and a very value-oriented person.

It was the '60s and I had just been diagnosed with schizophrenia. But in the '60s, instead of being known as severe, persistent mental illness, mental illness was known as a "nervous breakdown."

I was adjusting to having to take medicine and to living with a serious illness. I was working and going out with a girlfriend on Friday nights to local clubs, listening to music and dancing. It was a fun time.

One night a good-looking man approached and asked me to dance. He was very nice and seemed to have a good sense of humor. We went on to date, and eventually, we got engaged. During our engagement we had talked of my having had a nervous breakdown. This did not daunt my husband-to-be in the slightest, who did not suffer from mental illness. We eventually got married, and this is where my story begins.

What I did not know was that my upbringing by a single parent did not prepare me for the ins and outs of my marriage. The dinner parties and other entertaining, the endless cooking, the cleaning, and working full-time. Looking back, I think it was a perfect setting for someone to fail who was dealing with the effects of schizophrenia and side effects of medication. Most of the time in the early years of my marriage I was tired. I knew it was probably because of the medication, but that did not make me feel any better. Our social life continued and so did my working full-time.

I was so tired and unhappy with marriage in the first few years that I wanted to end the marriage before children came. I approached my husband and said, "I think I made a mistake. Marriage is too hard for me." He said, "Valerie, you can do it." I said, "It is not what I thought marriage would be." "Are you getting ill, Valerie?" he asked. Immediately I had fear sweep me. "No, I feel well," I said. "You know my psychiatrist thinks I am doing well." My husband had a very concerned look on his face, but I kept telling myself I had just seen my psychiatrist who was happy with my progress.

This article was published in the *Psychiatric Rehabilitation Journal,* 2001, 25(2), 196–198, and is reprinted with permission.

My husband left the room saying he had to make a telephone call. When he returned, he said, "Valerie, recently I have been looking into a new psychiatrist for you. I found one I think would be good for you. I just called him, and he wants you to go to the hospital."

"But I am fine mentally," I said. Now I was very frightened. This could not be happening—that I could be taken to a hospital against my will when I was fine, and my psychiatrist thought I was fine. And to have a new psychiatrist my husband chose instead of my choosing? My husband said, "If you don't come with me, I'll call the police." I said, "Call them, and I'll call my psychiatrist." The police came while I was on the phone with my psychiatrist, who again said he would see me during my next regular visit, not to worry. I relayed this information to the police officer and gave my psychiatrist's number. He said my husband had spoken to a psychiatrist who wanted me hospitalized, and I had to go with them. I was in terror by this time. My heart and mind were racing while I was trying to think what I could do. Unable to help myself, I was forced to go with them. This was the beginning of the end of my marriage. (This was the '60s, and there was no Screening Law to protect the mentally ill from situations such as I have described.)

When I returned home from the hospital, I was doing all I was supposed to almost in a daze. A joy in what I was doing was absent. I was feeling depressed and unhappy. Yet I was trying to make the marriage work since I didn't seem able to leave it. Our entertaining continued. I felt a stranger to many of our friends. I remember during one gathering, a friend of my husband's said, "I went by the looney bin in Morristown last week. Some of the crazies were walking on the grounds. You know, they should really keep these crazies locked inside." I felt an anger deep inside me, but I showed no emotion outwardly. I continued to have the proverbial ache, knowing if these people knew I suffered from mental illness, I would be ostracized.

A part of my illness during those years was having racing, upsetting thoughts most of the day and strong impulses along with these thoughts. I had a strong ally to go to who understood and could give me support and encouragement, and that was the new psychiatrist who treated me. Surprisingly, I had formed a therapeutic alliance. I felt I needed a stability that could not be questioned by my family, and my psychiatrist was this stability. Because of this alliance, I slowly started to be more independent, as long as I was able to run plans by him. It is sad I felt I had to do this, but I did after being forcibly removed from my home on my husband's word.

Then I became pregnant. I was apprehensive and a little frightened of the changes in my body. I never expressed my fears about pregnancy to anyone since I never heard other women say anything other than what a wonder pregnancy was. Finally, I gave birth to a beautiful daughter. My husband was an ecstatic father, and I was an ecstatic mother. This was my first experience of so deeply loving another human being aside from my mother. It gave me a strength I did not know I had. Our daughter was not a sleeper in the beginning of her life. Since my husband worked, I took care of our daughter during the day and at night. Again this was the '60s; and in the '60s, most men still did not share

> I continued to have the proverbial ache, knowing if these people knew I suffered from mental illness, I would be ostracized.

> I never expressed my fears about pregnancy to anyone since I never heard other women say anything other than what a wonder pregnancy was.

marital responsibilities other than working to support the family.

My mother was working full-time during this time and caring for my grandmother, so she could not stay with me to help me. After 6 months of day and night caring for my daughter, I was thoroughly exhausted and was hospitalized for a few weeks. I agreed to be hospitalized only after I knew my daughter was going to be taken care of by her grandmother, my husband's mother. While in the hospital, I thought of ways to conserve my strength so I

> ## I was always treated with care, never told upsetting things, and treated as a very frail, ill woman.

could try to make our marriage work. One solution was not to entertain so much and to have a more quiet lifestyle. My husband agreed. I was released from the hospital; and things were better for me at home. My extreme tiredness left me.

I then became pregnant a second time and gave birth to another little girl. This child was a sleeper and did not require the almost around-the-clock care. I was thoroughly happy with motherhood.

What also started happening was when family and close friends came to visit, I was always treated with care, never told upsetting things, and treated as a very frail, ill woman. I also saw a pattern developing in our marriage when we would have an argument. My illness would always be brought into it. One day I asked, "Why do you throw in my face the medical bills? I have gone to work part-time to pay for my hospitalization. I'm sorry I deal with mental illness, but you knew I did when I married you. I was honest with you," I finished. My husband said, "I'm sorry I say the things I do. I won't do it anymore." Until the next time, I thought.

I saw what my life would be like if I continued with my marriage. I saw that even my beloved daughters would see me as a sick, frail person and not the person I felt I could be. I never forgot my fear of

being removed from my home because I was saying things my husband did not think I should be saying. Because of my fear, I was always cautious of what I said and how I said it.

I thought a lot about my marriage. About whether to stay and continue to live in a hollow shell, continue to be a wife to a husband who did not understand the complexities of me as a person. I knew my husband would never leave me. But I knew, too, he enjoyed the role of caretaker of me with our close friends and family. "Why do you always just want me to stay home," I said to him one day. "I feel I have to grow, to be with other people, to find my potential and live up to it," I ended. My husband said, "I don't want you to get sick; I want you to stay calm and not to get so excited about things." I said, "I am a person, I feel fine, and I need to grow. Can you understand that?" I finished. My husband did not respond.

I believed very strongly I could become a whole person even with the illness. I had a very good psychiatrist, and I no longer resisted taking my medication. I thought of my options for about a year. I also continued to think about fulfilling my potential as a person or remaining the sickly, frail wife and mother. I felt very suffocated and decided to end the marriage. After very

> ## I believed very strongly I could become a whole person even with the illness.

careful thought and speaking with my psychiatrist, gaining his support if a custody battle developed, I said to my husband in the most gentle way, not bringing guilt or accusations into it, "Because of my illness, marriage is too hard for me. I have talked over ending my marriage with my doctor. He concurs I am not getting ill and further believes I will be able to be a good mother, caring for our children as a single parent which he'll testify to if need be." I continued, "I have seen a lawyer and want nothing for myself—only support for the children." My husband was expressionless and said, "Sounds like you have made your plans very carefully." "Yes, I am certain this is what I want," I said. Within a year our marriage ended.

My children thrived in our home and I thrived. I gained self-confidence. I worked full-time, had nice friends, and thoroughly enjoyed motherhood. In the evenings, we would take walks; I would bake often, cook favorite, nutritional meals, and teach the best values I knew to my children. Sometimes, for whatever unknown reason to me, my daughters would come rushing to me, throwing their arms around me, saying, "We love you, Mom." At these times, I did not doubt I could "conquer the world."

I also was vigilant about their education. In the second grade, my one little girl was having trouble learning to read. The school would not have her tested, saying the teacher thought there was no problem. I felt there was and scraped together the $250 to have her tested by a psychologist. The results were that my daughter had learning disabilities that the school then addressed, and my daughter did very well in school thereafter.

Single parenting is exhausting; when mental illness and medications are involved, it is even more daunting. Yet the rewards were tremendous. Deep inside myself, I was always afraid of the possibility I would become ill and the dread of what would happen. As the years passed, my fears abated—perhaps too much. In the years since my marriage ended, I did suffer one more tragic episode of schizophrenia that changed my life and my children's. They went to live with their father. It was heartbreaking for me and for them. When I got well, we reunited, and our love remains. Our present relationship took a lot of work, a lot of pain, but our love has endured.

I see other couples today that each deal with mental illness, and I wonder if it would have been different had I chosen a partner who also dealt with mental illness. I don't know. During the '60s, the psychiatrist I was seeing did not think it was a good idea to date other persons suffering from mental illness. He thought it better for me to integrate fully in the community.

I never married again. I did date for a few years after my divorce, but stopped. My life today is full.

Today I have a very good relationship with one of my daughters, and a less perfect, but good relationship with my other daughter. Each year, however, our bond as a family becomes stronger. I cherish this. I have friends both in the mental health system and out of it. I work full-time in the field of mental health, and I write articles and stories regarding mental illness. I live in a nice apartment, and I drive a decent car.

> My journey toward fulfillment was not attained by traveling a straight road, but rather a very winding road with many turns.

Since my childhood I always have wanted to be a writer and a caretaker of people. Today, I am a writer and a caretaker working with other persons suffering from mental illness. My journey toward fulfillment was not attained by traveling a straight road, but rather a very winding road with many turns. I believe I have reached my potential and certainly have found fulfillment. I am ever aware of new possibilities for myself and have never been sorry I left the "frail and sickly" woman behind.

photovoice

I found more
peace and serenity
than I had known
in years.

I call this "Twilight on the Lake." A group of us
from Fellowship Place went on a trip to a camp on
Paradox Lake in New York state. During the weekend
we spent there, I found more peace and serenity than
I had known in years. If I could wake up in this place
everyday, I believe I could overcome my depression.
—Helen, from *Wellness As I See It,* 2003

From Darkness to Light: From Turmoil to Serenity

Victoria E. Molta

For years, I retreated from the world by living within the deep recesses of my mind. I was like a frightened dog cowering in the darkness of a cave trying to avoid the sunlight because it was too searing. Now, I see the light in a different way. It appears warm and inviting, beckoning to me to come out of my cave in the forms of people's hands reaching out to me. I emerge from the darkness into the light.

For a long time, the world to me was like the wild sea. It was a dangerous, threatening place. The world rushed in like ocean waves washing onto the sand dunes of my mind. I was pulled in and dragged down to the bottom where creatures scuttled along the ocean floor. But, miraculously, I didn't die. Beneath the surface, I glided along and stillness engulfed me. Just then, I had a vision that the stillness was just like deeply felt serenity within one's soul. I sprang up from the sea and breathed in the cool, salt air, alive and renewed.

I have lived with a major mental illness for over half my life, since I was twenty years old. I consider myself a survivor of an inner battle that I waged for many years. The world to me was a threatening place, and I felt like a writhing snake with its skin torn off, baking under a hot desert sun. Every time I faced a challenge in my life, it was so unbearably painful that I retreated within myself. But the inner world was not safe either.

In fact, it was far more terrifying than the world outside me. Though I was tormented from the time of my childhood, I wasn't actually diagnosed with a severe mental illness until years later, when I was twenty-five years old. I believe my father, an alcoholic and still actively drinking, had been mentally ill for many years, but never diagnosed and treated for it. He medicated himself with booze. I believe he passed the illness on to me.

Stress plays a very important part in triggering either a manic or depressed episode. Moving from place to place were stressors that intensified my illness. I was twenty years old when my life began unraveling, and I found it increasingly difficult to function. I was a junior in college at the University of Vermont, a transfer student from a women's college in Boston. The stress of leaving my friends and starting over soon became unbearable. I had moved from place to place since I was a sophomore in high school, and my mother divorced my father and moved the four of us children from California to Connecticut. A year later, we moved to a small town over the state border into New York where I began my third high school in three years. After graduating, I attended the college in

> Every time I faced a challenge in my life, it was so unbearably painful that I retreated within myself. But the inner world was not safe either.

This article was published in the *Psychiatric Rehabilitation Journal*, 2002, 26(1), 97–98, and is reprinted with permission.

Boston for two years before transferring to the University of Vermont.

I learned to run from pain. But, the pain caught up with me eventually. Depression was the dominant aspect of my disease, although mania and thought disorders were mixed with it. In school, I trudged through snowdrifts five feet high to the library, where I attempted to study for hours. I couldn't concentrate or process the information and my mind buzzed like angry bees. I experienced physical pains in my side, and in the middle of the night, went to the emergency room. But, the doctors found nothing wrong. In attempts to escape from the increasingly dark, heavy curtain of despair that engulfed me, I went to the nearby discotheque and danced, drank, and slept with strangers. Anxiety threaded through my very existence. I pulled all my eyebrow hairs out. Before long, I had suicidal thoughts and felt an inner war wage inside me between wanting to live and graduate from college or die as a final solution to the madness. I was experienced in the psychosis of thought and mood disorders, though, at the time, I didn't know it. I slipped in and out of the punishing world within my mind; a world of self-hatred and distorted thoughts; a Technicolor world of visions, while the world outside was gray, hazy, unreal. Emotions were like blazing fires that I could not put out. Thoughts weren't reasonable or rational.

They were like the deafening sounds of a locomotive running through my head. Thoughts were noises, blasting music. Though rationality and reason were in the periphery of my mind like mountains in the distance, I managed to keep my eye on those mountains even when clouds obscured them.

Despite other crises that occurred the final two years of college—an abusive relationship, and living in Spain for four months as an exchange student with the psychosis intensifying to the point of terror, I managed to graduate from college and moved back to Boston.

For two years, the loud music within my mind ceased. My psychosis went into remission. Like clothes once thrown haphazardly from bureau drawers after a devastating earthquake, they were now folded and put neatly back into the drawers and closed up. My once crazy emotions were tucked away, and my rational thoughts dominated.

In my poem, I see the world as threatening like the wild sea or searing sunlight. But, the visions, sounds, delusions, despair, and mania within my mind were far more terrifying. Eventually, I would have to turn to the world and to people to save me from the inner havoc my mind created.

In 1986, at twenty-five years old, the illness returned. I checked myself into a mental hospital in Florida, which turned out to be a hellish experience, and was finally flown up to Connecticut to live with my mother and begin the long road to recovery.

I could run no more. I had to face the demons within as well as learn to trust people who reached their hands out to me. I attended a Psychiatric Day Hospital, moved into a Halfway House, and began the long journey back to sanity. Beneath the surface of my mind, stillness began to engulf me like deeply felt serenity within my soul. I put the pieces together. I needed the world and a support system of caring hands to stay well.

> I have returned from a long journey that took me away from the world for a while, but I am back.

2001! Fifteen years have passed since I was first diagnosed with a major mental illness. I am not cured, but I have been out of a locked psychiatric ward since 1988. I am happily married and have many friends. I am in recovery and am grateful for every day. I have returned from a long journey that took me away from the world for a while, but I am back.

Pivotal Therapeutic Moments:
A Patient's Perspective on Surviving Suicide

Terry L. Wise

I'm not sure, but I think my husband committed suicide. On December 25th, just 15 months later, I sat alone, cross-legged on our bed in the very spot I felt his last pulse. The day was going to become quite different than how I had customarily spent Christmas mornings. It was a day that now bears the distinction of my attempt to be the next in line. (pg. 10)

On Christmas day, 2000, I didn't just peer over the edge of a rooftop. I jumped off, feet airborne with the cement blocks of depression shackled to my ankles. The final thing I recall was swallowing the last fistful of Percocets. I did not make an attempt to commit suicide. I killed myself. (pg. 14)

—*Waking Up: Climbing Through the Darkness,*
by Terry L. Wise

On Christmas Day 2000, I swallowed 200 Percocets and 60 doses of Morphine with a pint of gin. Two days later, I woke up and found myself in ICU and then on the liver transplant floor of a Boston hospital. There is an enzyme in the liver called an ALT. The normal count for a healthy liver is 50. Mine was 18,000. Needless to say, how I survived still remains a medical mystery.

My body landed like an oak tree after receiving the final chop of a lumberjack's swing. Except for my cheek smashing against the floor, I have no recollection of first opening my eyes. The tile of the bathroom floor was the first thing I saw. I was completely anesthetized, fully incapable of feeling anything except the weight of my body as it

pounded the breath right out of me. A corpse with a pulse... (pg. 119)

Seconds, minutes, or perhaps hours later, I began to discern the shocking reality. Contrary to the laws of science, I was still alive, seated on the bathroom floor a few feet from my bed—an anatomical aberration that was nothing short of miraculous. One of my worst fears had become a reality. I had woken up from committing suicide. (pg. 120)

What preceded my suicide attempt was my husband's death.

Three weeks before our wedding, my husband, Peter, was diagnosed with ALS (Amyotrophic Lateral Sclerosis), otherwise known as Lou Gehrig's Disease. I must admit, this was one wedding gift I desperately wanted to return. Unfortunately, the hospital informed us that it was a final "sale."

ALS is a fatal, untreatable, neurological disease that causes progressive paralysis throughout a person's body, leaving the mind completely unaffected. Inevitably, within an average 2 to 5 years, its victims will literally become trapped inside a motionless body until they die.

The disease began with Peter's speech and quickly deprived him of the ability to speak intelligibly. Over the next 4 years, it took its course through the remainder of his body, ultimately claiming his life and leaving me as a 35-year-old widow. My suicide attempt occurred a year and a half after Peter's death.

Most people assumed that the reason for my attempt was Peter's death. There is no doubt that the

This article was published in the *Psychiatric Rehabilitation Journal*, 2004, 28(1), 88–92, and is reprinted with permission. The article includes excerpts from *Waking Up: Climbing Through the Darkness, 2004*, by Terry L. Wise, published by Pathfinder Publishing.

loss of my husband at such a young age was an enormous part of my depression. However, it wasn't necessarily his death as much as it was the consequences of 4 years of primary, full-time caregiving coupled with, as I later learned in treatment with a psychologist, the culmination of a number of earlier experiences I had during my life.

There is a general assumption that when a person survives a serious suicide attempt, they wake up feeling relieved to be alive. This is not necessarily the case.

> Scuba divers are instructed to follow the direction of their air bubbles if they ever become so disoriented that they can't figure out which way is up. I felt as though my oxygen tank had burst, and while I was frantically swimming upwards to the surface, I noticed that my air bubbles were going sideways.

> The doctors had assured me of a full recovery and the nausea had dissipated, but I was still weeks away from being out of the woods. Combined with the residue of poisons still floating through my body, unrelenting physical suffering had only compounded my despair. I knew I couldn't go back to making another attempt. I knew I couldn't go forward to a future of misery. I knew I could not remain where I was. Hopelessness was a ravenous predator on the psychological food chain, and it was swallowing me whole. (pg. 123)

Following my discharge from the hospital, I embarked on an aggressive course of therapy with a psychologist, Dr. Betsy Glaser. Treatment for my depression consisted of a number of things. First, it required a firm commitment to psychotherapy and actually making a consistent appearance in my therapist's office. Previously, I had kept one foot out the door during each appointment and continued to vacillate between whether or not I would return.

Second, "talk therapy" was combined with taking anti-depressant medication. I had been opposed to taking medication—mostly because of the stigma I had associated with anti-depressants. In time, and with the help of my therapist, I overcame various psychological barriers and began to take prescribed med-

ication. It became a tool that allowed me to become more present for the work we did during treatment.

> Ejected from death's cannon, the fingers of mortality had plucked me out of the tumble and flung me back into the chair at [Dr. Glaser's] office. Although I was still whirling in despair, my mind had clearly begun to increase its attendance. Fortunately, not only did I respond to the anti-depressant medication, but I was so ultra-sensitive that it only took days, rather than the norm of weeks, before I began to feel its subtle effects. It wasn't long before my years of stubborn resistance were eclipsed by the realization that I had suffered unnecessarily for so long. (pg. 138)

When I first began psychotherapy, I stubbornly refuted any connection between the past and the present and balked at anything that sounded like standard, textbook "psychobabble" or the "tell me about your mother" approach. But fortunately, I fell into the hands of a brilliant psychologist. After a lot of hard work together, it soon became undeniable that there was indeed a connection between my adult depression and childhood experiences. In fact, I began to recall thinking about wanting to die as young as 10 years old.

> [Dr. Glaser] continued to chip away at my protests that the past was not an integral factor in understanding the present. However, even to me, it became increasingly evident that we were trimming the top of a rapidly growing weed, rather than looking below, and pulling it out by its roots. (pg. 45)

More specifically, among many other significant, contributing factors, we began to explore the enduring impact of years of child sexual abuse at the hands of my stepfather and exposure to domestic violence.

> ...child abuse does not end when the touching stops... (A. Sidney Johnson III, President & CEO, Prevent Child Abuse America)

Although I had begun to accept some connection between childhood events and my depression, I continued to fill the mold of most child abuse victims by remaining firmly convinced that I was almost entirely responsible. I even opposed the use of the term "abuse" during our sessions. In my unwavering opinion, what had occurred could not be defined as "abuse" since, among other reasons I steadfastly held onto, my stepfather's actions weren't accompanied by threats or violence—or so I thought. There were no reasons to see things otherwise, only excuses. Blame, shame, and self-loathing consumed me.

> "I already know everything there is to know. I lived it. I understand it. I am not going to dwell on my past, or cop out with a victim-of-child-abuse claim..." I retorted. (pg. 55)

Dr. Glaser faced the arduous task of prying loose 25 years of self-condemnation. Through methodical, exhaustive questioning, she patiently explained the importance of re-creating "the context."

We discussed a variety of factors that I had previously overlooked. These included the intimidating and violent atmosphere in my house when I was a child. I had suffered intense loneliness, and I had entertained thoughts of suicide by the time I reached the fourth grade. Slowly, Dr. Glaser and I assembled pieces of a puzzle that soon formed a picture I hadn't seen before. My stubborn resistance began to give way to a new twist of logic: I had suffered the consequences of having been sexually abused.

> As best as I was able, it was the very beginning of understanding the concept of remembering things without an adult mindset. I needed to put myself back into the atmosphere as a 10-year-old, without the choices, knowledge, or life experiences of an adult. After months of work, I was still unconvinced. Yet, I started to entertain the notion that what I knew at 35 was not what I knew when I was 10. This was the first time I ever recalled being presented with logical and valid reasons to support a different perspective about the liabilities of my childhood. (pg. 62)

My depression was compounded by the effects of long-term caregiving. During the last year of my husband's life, and prior to my suicide attempt, I was in treatment with Dr. Glaser for a brief period of time.

Since the moment Peter was diagnosed with Lou Gehrig's Disease, I had been reborn into an entirely new body of indescribable agony. I never saw my former self again. Regardless of where we went, we would never again be without the company of our new, unwanted stalker—the random, indeterminate path of ALS that slowly deprived Peter of his speech, movement, and ultimately his life.

I knew I had become desensitized to many of the adjustments I had unconsciously made during the slow progression of Peter's illness. But I had treated fatigue like a nuisance, not an obstacle. My hands worked, so I could shave him. My mouth worked, so I could speak for him. My arms worked, so I could lift him. My legs worked, so I could bring him the things he needed.

Initially, I went to see Dr. Glaser because I feared that I was having a nervous breakdown. Sadly, I wasn't concerned for myself. I was afraid I would become incapacitated and therefore, unable to care for my husband.

As I elaborated upon the conditions of my life, Dr. Glaser began to urge me to seek outside help with Peter's care. I refused. Peter and I already had begun to perpetuate the classic self-destructive cycle that occurs between a patient and caregiver, and typically among spouses. He insisted that I do everything for him and refused all outside help, and I couldn't justify doing anything less.

Peter required my full-time care. His speech was unintelligible, and I had become his full-time interpreter. He could no longer eat without assistance or constant choking. He could no longer walk, drive, or bathe himself. I was sleep deprived from being on call and turning him throughout the night. I was managing the medical bills and every other task of our lives. Many of Peter's needs were highly personal, and I

> I learned that even though there were periods of time when I would feel better, it was understandable, and maybe even expected, that the suicidal feelings would continue to periodically return.

couldn't fathom exacerbating the indignities he suffered on a daily basis by forcing him to accept assistance from an outsider.

During one of our sessions, Dr. Glaser made a statement that caused a profound shift in my perspective. She said, "Terry, just because you can physically do all of these things, does *not* mean you can do them psychologically."

Never before had it occurred to me that there could be psychological reasons for needing help with Peter's care. Until that moment, as long as I was still standing, any notion of seeking help for his care had been inexcusable to me. I had never considered the intricate link between my physical and emotional capacities. Time had fostered an inverse relationship between our needs. As Peter's condition required more of me, my strength and stamina had steadily declined. His disease had been progressing, taking my will to live right along with it.

With Dr. Glaser's help, I was able to realize that Peter and I had both become guilty of creating unreasonable expectations of me. As I began to recognize some of my human limitations, I was able to enlist the help of others for some of his care.

> I had a million justifications for bottling up any notions of self-interest. But they would no long withstand my new awareness. (pg. 36)

Unfortunately, not enlisting the help of others and not seeking that advice sooner almost cost me my life. After my husband's death, and what seemed like several lifetimes later, I attempted suicide.

Regretfully, as Peter's condition declined, I chose to leave therapy. Despite Dr. Glaser's conviction that she could help me further, I was too clouded to see how I could have benefited from remaining in treatment. What I didn't realize until much later, when I returned to psychotherapy, was that while I could not have done anything to control the course of Peter's illness, there were many things I could have done to control its impact.

Depression is a spectrum disorder. Oftentimes, it is the result of a number of experiences rather than a single event. Working with Dr. Glaser opened the gateway to unearthing a breadth of issues underlying my depression, including the consequences of long-term caregiving, child abuse, loss, suicidality, and bereavement.

> Our work continued forward like psychological archeology, as if the roots of my every emotion were being unearthed and dusted off with her feather brush. (pg. 147)

During the weeks following the attempt, I began to make some positive changes that broke the self-destructive pattern I had been living in for years. For example, I began to take anti-depressant medication, I stopped drinking alcohol and taking painkillers, and I re-learned normal sleeping and eating habits, which, after 4 years of primary caregiving for my husband, I had completely neglected. Consequently, over time, I was more *present* for the work we did during treatment and more receptive to positive emotions.

> My increased understanding about the course of my depression, as well as the trust we had established in our relationship, enabled me to risk telling her these feelings without the fear that she would panic and seek immediate hospitalization.

However, *even then*, I learned it was going to be a long process before I came out of my suicidal despair. This was a critical lesson. Over the course of many sessions with Dr. Glaser, I learned that even though there were periods of time when I would feel better, it was understandable, and maybe even expected, that the suicidal feelings would continue to periodically return. Most importantly, I learned that this did not mean I was back at the bottom again. This cycle of emotions was part of the process of recovering—not necessarily a relapse into a suicidal depression.

Understanding that it was acceptable for me to have this periodic despair was critical and helped me in several ways. First, it helped me to realize that just because I was feeling depressed again, didn't mean I was destined to inevitable misery—something I had previously believed—and that feelings of happiness weren't just fleeting moments that I would never be able to hold onto.

Second, Dr. Glaser was able to point out that the volatility of my emotions was evidence that I was feeling ups as well as downs—and those were periods of progress that I had previously overlooked.

Third, it gave me permission to talk to Dr. Glaser about how depressed I was *still* feeling—which, particularly after an attempt, is very scary because whoever knows that you've already made an attempt, knows that you might mean business. It was that ability to talk about my post-attempt suicidal feelings with Dr. Glaser that led to another very critical lesson, which I now refer to as "breaking down the swirl."

During one of our sessions, I told Dr. Glaser that I was feeling like I wanted to die again. I felt overwhelmed by "everything." My increased understanding about the course of my depression, as well as the trust we had established in our relationship, enabled me to risk telling her these feelings without the fear that she would panic and seek immediate hospitalization. She continued to ask me why I felt like dying, and I kept replying that it was because of a "swirl of things." It had become almost habitual for me to just lump everything together as one mass of misery or pain.

Dr. Glaser made a statement that caused a pivotal shift in my thinking. She said, in effect, that unless we figured out what fears and anxieties comprised that "swirl," I would always continue to live in a pattern of "jumping to the dying part" without first thinking through what was so overwhelming to me. Never before had I realized that this was a pattern of mine.

Dr. Glaser went on to suggest that suicide was my escape route and therefore, it was understandable that I would feel like I wanted to die during periods of

stress. Suicide had become a door that I needed to know still could be opened. But that didn't mean it was okay to open or walk through it. It just explained part of the reasons why suicide was still such a prevalent thought. It had become a coping mechanism of mine. It was a means by which I escaped from dealing with my underlying emotions. I wasn't consciously avoiding my feelings. I just didn't have the tools to know how to stop and take a look at them. All of these lessons permitted me to speak with Dr. Glaser about my continued anguish.

> I came to understand that there was no defined formula for treatment, and that it was a work in progress, with victories and setbacks along the way.

During the ensuing months of our sessions, I learned about the next step in the therapeutic process—how to break down the "swirl." Dr. Glaser asked me to pick one thing, anything, that was bothering me. This gave us the opportunity to identify, dissect, and examine each feeling of despair I was having—and to understand the emotional domino effect that was occurring.

For example, I finally explained that part of my distress was caused by the fear that I would fail at my new job. Putting aside the issues we later dealt with about what was behind my lack of self-esteem, divulging this fear led into a discussion about how upset I was that, at 35 years old, I felt like I was starting all over again. This exacerbated how alone I felt and triggered more grief about the loss of my husband.

It feels like [my husband] was given a death sentence, and now, I've been given a life sentence. (pg. 41)

Discussing those feelings led to talking about my feelings of "painful envy." I was painfully envious of other couples who had their health and their future together. But then I disliked myself for not wishing them well, and for not always being happy for the people I cared about. This, in turn, led to feeling self-hatred for not being more appreciative of what I did have. The crucial importance of breaking down my feelings became evident.

Further into treatment, I learned that many of my feelings could co-exist. I could feel both happy for others and pained about my predicament. I learned that my envy didn't preclude how much I cared about other people, nor did it make me a bad person. In turn, these discussions opened the door to talking about the pain I felt over the loss of my husband—and accepting that my fears and loneliness were the normal consequences of losing a spouse, particularly at such a young age. Because of my preoccupation with suicide, I hadn't even really begun to grieve his death, yet.

In essence, "breaking down the swirl" led to talking about my feelings in more detail—feeling them and understanding them so that they would eventually feel less painful. As a result of understanding myself better, I was able to withstand a lot more of the difficult feelings I was having—so I didn't always "jump to the dying part."

> It would be a long while before I was out of the woods, but the cadence of insightfulness had begun to shift, leading us to a more promising clearing. Even if I didn't like what I first saw, I was much more comfortable with beginning to know myself, rather than continuing to live without explanations for my unhappiness. (pg. 153)

> I soon accepted that I had been traveling throughout my life on a freight train filled with a personal gang of monsters—monsters of loneliness, anxiety, fear and destructive self-images. With an increasingly receptive stance, each new understanding unloaded another unwelcome passenger, making room for the new companions on my journey. (pg. 192)

I continued to experience "therapeutic moments"—that is, periods of time when I was able to see things with a new set of eyes. I began to view the therapeutic process as a whole, rather than a succession of isolated appointments. Each session was a sequel to the last. I came to understand that there was no defined formula for treatment, and that it was a work in progress, with victories and setbacks along the way.

I learned that there was a course of depression. And even today I still feel periods of time when I'm very depressed—and sometimes, I still struggle with suicidal feelings. However, I now understand that this does not mean I'm back to that horrible place, stuck and unable to move forward in any direction. I have learned that even during the times I don't feel good about my life or myself, I still can feel hopeful. I know that my feelings of despair won't be forever and equally as important, that in the meantime, I don't have to be alone with them.

And with these pivotal lessons, I hope to present myself as a *living* example of how the therapeutic process can work to keep hope—and people—alive.

My sense of
humor is my
greatest
survival asset.

"Sugar Mamas" is a candy store in Newtonville. I
know this sign should offend me as a mental patient,
but it doesn't. I like it and it makes me smile. My
sense of humor is my greatest survival asset. Life has
made me tough, and I don't sweat the dopey stuff.
Trying to do the right thing is hard, and I expend my
energies on that and not on stupid, trivial stuff. Everyone likes to go nuts in a fun way every now and then,
and if it's all in good fun, I say "go nuts."

—Michelle, from *Taking Off the Blinders*, 2005

Hearing Voices and Seeing Pictures

J. P. Lee

My senses are functioning well, expressing keenness in sight, smell, taste, touch, and hearing. However, I notice that I am aware of some additional stimuli which originate, are developed, and are perceived in the mind. I am referring to auditory hallucinations, visual hallucinations, and thought disorder. At worst, they can lead to confusion, delusions, and inappropriate behavior. They may elicit emotions, feelings, and reactions that are not the usual response to the real external influence that the five senses are picking up. There may be a separation from my reality. This mental breakdown can lead to physical problems. The presence of the hallucinations and other positive symptoms, and the mental and physical breakdown, the negative symptoms, establishes the pathological state of my schizophrenia (Torrey, 1995; Weiden, Scheifler, Diamond & Ross, 1999).

Having schizophrenia, I am concerned about the deterioration of cognitive functions and the impact of medication I need for treatment. Left untreated, hallucinations can overpower a person, and the symptoms become a part of the person's repertoire. They can affect my ability to pay attention, concentrate, solve a problem, make judgmental calls, and other mental abilities.

The symptoms of mental illness in the time before the mid 1990s were alleviated by conventional antipsychotic medications. These medications usually caused heavy sedation, physical discomfort, and mental impairment. Although alleviating me of some of the disruptive voices, I am then faced with other physical deficits. In the course of my illness, I was treated with many of the conventional medications. In the 1990s, atypical antipsychotic medications with lesser side effects have been introduced to replace the older medications. These include rispiradol, and olanzapine which I took, and clozapine and others.

Since side effects of medication cause a decline in my mental capacity, the question, "What is a state of well being?" needed to be addressed. Treatment will vary from individual to individual. It is important that both the psychiatrist and family of a patient like myself recognize in the treatment of hallucinations two goals. One goal is to eliminate psychosis including delusional thinking. The other goal is to appreciate the presence of other legitimate mental processes such as spiritualism, mysticism, or psychic experiences. Prescribing the most effective level of medication to be used for treatment is critical to achieving this balance. I have to be relieved of the

> Left untreated, hallucinations can...affect my ability to pay attention, concentrate, solve a problem, make judgmental calls, and other mental abilities.

This article was published in the *Psychiatric Rehabilitation Journal*, 2005, 29(1), 73–76, and is reprinted with permission.

harshness of troublesome hallucinations and delusional thoughts. However, I do not want to be overmedicated and impoverished of mental functions.

Fortunately, throughout my illness, I was treated only at doses of medication on the lower end of the dose scale. I have not suffered any permanent mental deterioration. Presently, although on medication, I am still left with residual hallucinations which I have to adapt to. Different approaches can be used to cope with hallucinations. These include passive illness behavior, passive problem solving, active problem solving, active problem avoiding, symptomatic coping and other coping (Escher, Romme, Buiks, Delespaul & Van Os, 2002). Using cognitive behavioral therapy (CBT), active problem solving, I had a powerful tool to rely on, to think clearly, and remain autonomous to the hallucinations (Lafond, 1993–2005). I also learned to adapt to thoughts that were a challenge to live with.

CBT offers a process to reverse the confusion caused by hallucinations, delusions, or thought disorder. When I was initially afflicted with such psychotic episodes two decades ago, I had not learned about the practice of CBT. Although medication relieved me of most of the symptoms of illness, I still had not come to terms with the problems caused by the confusing thoughts. CBT examines three steps of information processing: 1) stimulation by the hallucination or thought disorder, 2) the interpretation and reaction to the stimulus, 3) the consequence of the reaction. The steps are analyzed and the disruptive sequence revised. It may mean going over and changing step 2 until in step 3 the person's distress is relieved.

I will attempt to describe two scenarios. The first involves a stimulus which may bring inappropriate behavior, and the second scenario where I used CBT to modify the sequence of reactions of the first scenario. My stimulating problematic thought may be that I am suspicious that my friends may be secretly criticizing and ridiculing me and doing that in my presence using cryptic language with each other. My interpretation is that my friends don't really like me, and my reaction is one of resentment of this behavior. The consequence is that I am angry at my friends and

choose not to socialize so much with them. Having recognized this pattern, I now attempt CBT. I will respond to step 1 with a different interpretation and reaction for step 2.

> I have to be relieved of the harshness of troublesome hallucinations and delusional thoughts. However, I do not want to be overmedicated and impoverished of mental functions.

I will consider as a real possibility that my friends have not been ridiculing me using cryptic language. I will try harder not to sink into my paranoia, but instead talk and interact with them and engage more enthusiastically with the activities at hand. Step 3 is now different from the previous. The consequence is that I am no longer angry but more in synchrony with my friends. Having done one CBT exercise, I can mentally rehearse my way through future potential problematic/delusional thought in order to bypass the ravages of paranoid thinking. The next time when such stimuli trigger my mind, I can quickly recognize the pattern and change step 2 to relieve myself of confusion and harmful emotions. Hence, I am in charge of my symptoms. I am free from the strangulation of mental processes by excessive medication, and I am also free from the control of delusional thoughts.

It has been pointed out that whether a person views his voices as malevolent or benevolent, powerful or benign, depends on interpersonal relations. The social rank and power between the person and his social world influences the rank and power with the voice and thus determines his subordination or insubordination to the voice (Birchwood, Meaden, Trower, Gilbert & Pliastow, 2000). Entrapment by the voices in this way shows through contrast the importance of autonomy from the influence of voices in the thinking process. My goal then is to regulate my own self identity and be independent from the voice.

CBT is just one way to cope with voices. Strategies including other clinical interventions, behaviors specifically targeting voices, and general approaches to mental health that help in coping with voices have been documented as methods recommended to deal with the plight of hearing voices (Ritsher, Lucksted, Otilingam & Grajales, 2004). Overall, schizophrenia challenges cognitive functions. The frequency, volume, and nature of the voices I am faced with are variable, and therefore, my mental processes involving attention, concentration, and memory are put to the test accordingly, all the time. In addition to just confronting the mental deficits brought on by the different aspects of the disease, I also can actively avoid deterioration of the mind through apathy, and still learn and grow mentally over my lifetime, as healthy people would. Deliberate mental activity such as reading, watching TV, listening to music, playing a musical instrument, participating in sports, developing a hobby enables me to refocus and sharpen the mind.

> Whether a person views his voices as malevolent or benevolent, powerful or benign, depends on interpersonal relations.

CBT enables me to use some aspects of intellectual reasoning. More likely, these abilities can be enhanced upon by actively participating in intellectually stimulating academic study, leisure reading, or work. Perhaps it was just that I enjoyed academic work, that I spent many years of my adult life in academic studies, mostly at the university level. My BSc and MSc were completed before I had the first symptoms of illness. I also was able to work at the university as a lab tech and teaching assistant. Initially, as I set into my career and later to develop my career by going back to school, I found that I was faced with problems studying effectively. The sedative effects and discomfort brought on by the medication is very distracting, as many psychiatry patients know. The mind was very weak in its ability to focus and concentrate and think, and the willpower to do so, waning. Eventually, I pushed harder to read more. I often chose to read and study as an alternative to letting my mind wander idly, or even watch TV. Over the years, I developed some resilience, and I noticed that I have become able to focus quickly and even think better. I also was aware that the voices don't prevent me from learning, if my intention was to further myself intellectually.

I presently work as a math and science tutor. I find that the voices do distract me. I often need to reemphasize in my mind or rethink ideas or procedures, such as routine daily duties, if I didn't jot it down on paper to reinforce my memory. For other more elaborate ideas as those that are part of my work, I often write down my study notes and calculations to mentally rehearse things or even memorize before the actual tutoring. Sometimes, I write for another reason. Many times, thoughts that I may be preoccupied with in my mind have sparked some inspired or novel idea for me. Therefore I take time to write this down, usually on the computer so that I may read these words again and develop them further on another day. I had over the years done much thinking about many concepts in all sorts of topics. It is an attempt to recover control of the thinking process which is challenged by the presence of the voices.

> Deliberate mental activity such as reading, watching TV, listening to music, playing a musical instrument, participating in sports, developing a hobby enables me to refocus and sharpen the mind.

I use another powerful resource to control my thoughts. When my emotions are frayed by disruptive hallucinations, I've always used music appreciation to calm myself. When I listen to music, my mind is free from the unwanted thoughts and can momentarily avoid being carried away by inappropriate emotions. Sometimes, I sing with the music that I am listening to. I have even learned to play music on my clarinet or classical guitar. My music has improved, and I derive a sense of joy in being able to translate the notes on the music sheets to delightful sounds.

> **When my emotions are frayed by disruptive hallucinations, I've always used music appreciation to calm myself.**

Sports are another activity that I find essential for its role in offering relief from mental frustration. In doing so, sports have the attribute of building character. I participate in running, swimming, hiking, cross-country skiing, skating, canoeing, and squash. These sports not only take me out of the home for an adventure, but make me feel good by elevating the levels of painkillers, such as endorphins and encephalins in the bloodstream. It has been shown that the blood glucose level correlates with behavior and performance (Sharkey, 1990). The brain and nervous systems depend entirely on glucose as an energy source. Anxiety, nervousness, and fatigue, symptoms of individuals who are hypoglycemic are caused by the low levels of blood glucose. It is reported that fitness training improves an individual's ability to mobilize and metabolize fat, helping to conserve blood glucose that the brain needs. Almost any sport is initially hard work, especially for people with schizophrenia. It requires courage, willpower, concentration, and persistence. Aside from the fact that sports are fun and emotionally uplifting, they can promote building strength, finesse, and agility, both physically and men-

tally. Also, I suffer tremor and restlessness or akathisia as the side effects of the medication. Sports enable me to work on the muscles, and after a workout, I am more relaxed.

Early on, I acknowledged that my illness is long-term and chronic. By now, I am encouraged by doctors to take the recommended treatment of medication, employ CBT, and coaxed to make use of my own strategies. For the most part, I did not delay, but invested in my life activities. They include sports, hobbies, work, social interests, academic study, and volunteer work that I do at environmental organizations and at Church. I am also a member of the Schizophrenia Program Consumer Advisory Committee at the Royal Ottawa Hospital. However, there was still no suggestion by my doctors that by following these routes there would be a cure. Schizophrenia may be an environmentally triggered illness for those who may be genetically predisposed. Scientists have been reported to be examining specific genes for their role in causing this disease. However, my social worker, who is a certified cognitive behavioral therapist, suggested that even if I have information on the gene that

> **Aside from the fact that sports are fun and emotionally uplifting, they can promote building strength, finesse, and agility, both physically and mentally.**

caused my illness or had the brain scans to indicate what area of the brain was affected, I was really no better off, if there was no effective treatment plan for me. CBT presently is deemed a relatively new method that is powerfully effective in treating schizophrenia, and a lot of emphasis is given to support treatment procedures. There is still no "magic bullet" to cure schizophrenia, as antibiotics, like penicillin, were considered the "magic bullet" for curing many infectious diseases.

This year I went to a talk at the Royal Ottawa Hospital where I listened to a talk by Dr. M. Farkas from the Center for Psychiatric Rehabilitation at Boston University who uses the methods of psychosocial therapy. For the first time I am hearing that recovery is an attainable goal. Recovery is meant in the context of being able to function mentally and physically well and being able to adjust again in the social, work, or school settings with the standards established and being acknowledged as acceptable in each setting. In this context, the adjustments are not necessarily made at the level of improving the client's mind, but also at the workings at the societal level. For example, there is a move towards advocating for help for clients with mental illness at the post secondary level of education (Smiderle, 2003). There is so much stigma that a lot of work needs to be done in the person's environment so that he can be functional or accepted again in society. Dr. Farkas says that recovery just doesn't involve the head up, but also the whole of the person. Each person needs an individual path for his recovery as each is mentally skilled, socially skilled, financially adept, spiritually driven, differently.

In my own situation, my doctor doesn't request that total elimination of voices from my mind is necessary. Using the above mentioned strategies, I have reached the stage where I am considered as one who is pretty well adjusted back into my environment. The condition of hearing voices is tolerable if the person can live normally in his environment while he copes successfully with the problems (Romme & Escher, 1989). Regarding residual voices, I have struggled with the question as to what type of experience I am dealing with. Scientists have distinguished the similarities and differences between verbal hallucinations heard by people who have schizophrenic psychosis and those by college students who have normal consciousness. It is accepted that verbal hallucinations are a normal feature of consciousness for some proportion of a general population (Barrett & Caylor, 1998). People who have non-psychiatric medical conditions also can experience verbal hallucinations (Ritsher et al., 2004). Also, these scientists point out that verbal hallucinations can result from situational stress, cultural influences, meditation, and spiritual communication. I brought the topic to the attention of the hospital chaplain and a hospital social worker. In addition to having a pathological brain illness, schizophrenia, I also am experiencing connectedness with God and Extra Sensory Perception (ESP) with other human beings.

Spiritually, I communicate with God through prayer and thoughts of the divine at work. My spirituality is usually not through a voice that tells me of Him in my mind. It is usually a realization that some event in my life or idea in my mind is Holy and brought on by Him. Also, in my experience I have witnessed the omnipotence of God through His power of telekinesis, the movement of objects in and out of my home. Surprisingly, sometimes I am told of a future event. It comes as a message in the mind that is verified in reality. I become more aware of the Presence of the Lord in everything, everywhere in the universe, His omnipresence. Mysticism is at work as I am spiritually uplifted to God when I ponder at the beauty of creation of life on earth or at the far reaches of the universe. I point out that I worship God at Church and have participated in many bible studies.

The psychic phenomenon or ESP takes place in my mind when voices tell me what someone else is saying or doing. Some of my ESP thoughts have been validated by media and Internet news and informa-

> Although I live with schizophrenia, I also am gifted with the richness that comes with the inner spiritual and mystical experiences and with the excitement and challenges that accompany all of life's activities.

tion and personal communication, and therefore, taken into the context of reality.

In summary, although I live with schizophrenia, I also am gifted with the richness that comes with the inner spiritual and mystical experiences and with the excitement and challenges that accompany all of life's activities.

References

Barrett, T. R. & Caylor, M. R. (1998).Verbal hallucinations in normals, v: Perceived reality characteristics. *Personality and Individual Differences, 25*, 209–221.

Birchwood, M., Meaden, A., Trower, P., Gilbert, P. & Pliastow, J. (2000). The power and omnipotence of voices: Subordination and entrapment by voices and significant others. *Psychological Medicine, 30*, 337–344.

Escher, S., Romme, M., Buiks, A., Delespaul, P., Van Os, J. (2002). Independent course of childhood auditory hallucinations: A sequential 3-year follow-up study. *British Journal of Psychiatry, 181*(43), 10–18.

Farkas, M. (2004) Personal communication.

Lafond, V. (1993–2005) Personal communication.

Ritsher, J. B., Lucksted, A., Otilingam, P. G. & Grajales, M. (2004). Hearing voices: Explanations and implications. *Psychiatric Rehabilitation Journal, 27* (3), 219–227.

Romme, M. A. J., & Escher, A. (1989). Hearing voices. *Schizophrenia Bulletin, 15*(2), 209–216.

Sharkey, B. J. (1990). *Physiology of fitness*. Champaign, Illinois: Human Kinetics Books.

Smiderle, W. (2003). Higher education. *Schizophrenia Digest,* Winter, 28–30.

Torrey, E. F. (1995). *Surviving schizophrenia: A manual for families, consumers, and providers*. New York: Harper Collins Publishers Inc.

Weiden, P. J., Scheifler, P. L., Diamond, R. J., Ross, R. (1999). *Breakthroughs in antipsychotic medications*. New York: W.W. Norton & Company.

I...think of it as
self-soothing, or
being good to
yourself.

I have here a picture of Bostix in Copley Square
where you can purchase halfprice tickets for various
events throughout the city. This is also a reminder
that there are other discounts and even free events in
the city for example museums, matinees, and theater
performances. For me, using these means often are
rewarding, and it's part of my wellness recovery.
When I'm not at my best, it puts me in the moment
and usually I enjoy myself. When I am feeling well,
enjoyment is a given. I also think of it as self-soothing,
or being good to yourself.

—Gloria, from *Wellness As I See It,* 2003

A Wellness Approach

Margaret Swarbrick

The paradigm shift toward recovery was initiated by Anthony (1991, 1993, 2000) and first-person accounts written by a prominent mental health consumer leader (Deegan, 1988). Recovery is a deeply personal, unique process of (re)gaining physical, spiritual, mental, and emotional balance when one encounters illness, crisis, or trauma. As a process, the individual learns to accept the illness, crisis, or trauma and its associated challenges while adjusting attitudes, beliefs, and sometimes both life roles and goals. For some people, recovery is the ability to work, to live in housing of one's own choice, to have friends and intimate relationships, and to become a contributing member of one's community. Recovery, therefore, is a process of healing and restoring health and wellness during episodes of illness and life stressors.

Wellness is a conscious, deliberate process that requires a person to become aware of and make choices for a more satisfying lifestyle (Johnson, 1986; Swarbrick, 1997). Wellness is the process of creating and adapting patterns of behavior that lead to improved health in the wellness dimensions and heightened life satisfaction (Johnson, 1986). A wellness lifestyle includes a balance of health habits, such as adequate sleep and rest, productivity, exercise, participation in meaningful activity, nutrition, productivity, social contact, and supportive relationships (Swarbrick, 1997). Wellness is holistic and multi-dimensional, and includes physical, emotional, intellectual, social, environmental, and spiritual dimensions. Wellness approaches for mental health practice have been proposed in recent years (Copeland, 2002; Copeland & Mead, 2004; Hutchinson, 1996; Moller & Murphy, 1997; Swarbrick, 1997; Weed, 1999).

The notion of wellness generates internal motivation and active participation in a person's treatment so that he or she can learn to manage problems and stress (Swarbrick, 1997) in order to prevent a crisis situation and, possibly, in-patient hospitalization. The treatment of diabetes is a useful analogy to maintaining wellness when a person has a psychiatric diagnosis. Management of diabetes, like a diagnosis of mental illness, involves choosing and committing to a daily routine of medication, exercise, adequate nutrition, sleep and wake cycles, and rest (Swarbrick, 1997). This lifestyle pattern allows a person to maintain a level of physiological balance that impacts his or her physical, social, spiritual, and emotional well-being. A focus on health, strengths, and personal responsibility rather than dependence and illness can engender optimism and a belief in the capacity to exert personal control in managing total health needs.

There are some major differences between the medical model and the wellness approach. The med-

> Recovery...is a process of healing and restoring health and wellness during episodes of illness and life stressors.

This article was published in the *Psychiatric Rehabilitation Journal,* 2006, 29(4), 311–314, and is reprinted with permission.

ical model narrowly focuses on symptom reduction, rapid stabilization, and interventions focused on deficiencies and incapacity. In this deficit-based approach, individuals are seen in terms of their illness; what is often overlooked are people's interests, skills, abilities, and potential to achieve personal goals. The narrow focus on limitations often exacerbates the mental illness or crisis rather than supporting recovery.

The wellness approach, on the other hand, identifies goals, preferences, interests, and strengths of the individual. Wellness centers on health, whereas the medical model focuses on illness or disease management. This approach provides opportunities for persons to assume or resume the valued social roles necessary to achieve a decent quality of life. Wellness engenders a positive attitude rather than focusing on problems and issues.

> The wellness approach… identifies goals, preferences, interests, and strengths of the individual.

This perspective sparks internal motivation and strengthens an optimistic attitude. An individual is empowered to manage life crises and stress and direct his or her attention to wellness lifestyle goals.

The wellness approach outlines seven dimensions and their interrelated connections, which constitute the whole person. The concept of spirituality, for example, is metaphysical and, therefore, difficult to define objectively. Spirituality may be interpreted in terms of wellness as spiritual health, the extent to which a person's need for spiritual expression and growth are met. Spirituality is considered a strength, through its value as a contribution to health and healing. The medical model often excludes attention to the spiritual dimension, more often diagnosing the embracement of the spiritual dimension as a form of pathology, shamanism, ritualistic behavior, or quackery (Swarbrick & Burkhardt, 2000).

In the wellness approach, a person is empowered to assume personal responsibility and be proactive in the preservation of his or her own health. People are given an active role and responsibilities to self-monitor their own health behaviors and increase activity in the dimension where they perceive there is an imbalance. The motivation for compliance or adherence and commitment to change in the wellness approach comes through personal control and good health, whereas in the medical model, fear is used to drive change and instill compliance or adherence (Swarbrick, 1997). If one operates on the basis of fear, then the biological reaction to that fear can have a negative physiological and psychological effect on the body. This may compromise the interaction and deter positive change and healing.

A key to both the medical model and wellness approach is to help an individual to restore emotional and physical equilibrium by establishing and maintaining a predictable routine. A self-defined daily routine can help offset inner chaos and provides a pattern that helps a person to regain control and order in his or her life. It is important to make positive health choices while exerting control over events in their self-care routines, life, and participation in the community. The Wellness Recovery Action Plan (Copeland, 1997) provides an excellent strategy to help people develop daily plans and other self-awareness processes to help restore personal wellness and recovery.

I have a strong belief in the power of the wellness rather than the illness approach. My road to recovery has been long and winding and I continue my path to wellness, thankfully equipped with many more supports, skills, and a better attitude than when I started.

Twenty-eight years ago I encountered the mental health system as an adolescent. Instead of spending my freshman year in high school, I spent my time receiving long-term in-patient and out-patient services. High school was a nightmare and a blur because I never became fully integrated. I struggled to graduate, and I had no ambition for any career or life path. My sense of future was nonexistent. I had no personal goals and life dreams. I constantly wanted to return to the solace and safety of a hospital institution. Through anger, frustration, and anxiety, I developed a wellness vision of trying to look at myself as a whole person, including emotional, physical, social, occupational, spiritual, environmental, and intellectual dimensions. Initially, this kept me alive, and now it has helped me live each day more fully.

I continue to struggle with the many residual aspects of dealing with an emotional imbalance. Fortunately, I have been able to focus on my own wellness through swimming, employment, and pursuing education and training, which has empowered me to move forward to achieve personal goals—one step at a time. I found my way out of the hospital into other types of institutions, such as community college and work. I made slow and steady gains toward defining my occupational role in society. I did work many less than minimum wage jobs, and work became an adaptive obsession. I discovered that showing up for work was "half the battle." Work challenged me to get out of my head, cast aside daily rituals, overcome constant self-doubt, and do something for someone else. Work also provided a financial reward, which helped me break away from my perceived control by family and others. I developed several miserly skills that have served me well over the years and have helped me attain financial stability.

> Swimming has helped relieve serious bouts of depression and helped with clearing my thinking patterns.

Even though I have acknowledged my illness, I still can get caught up in its negativity, but I try to pay more attention to my overall wellness (physical health, emotional maturity, spirituality, living and working environment, intellectual capacity, and social supports) rather than the label of having been diagnosed with a mental illness.

Swimming has been the most critical tool in my arsenal of wellness tools that help keep me focused on my personal recovery. Early on it was an activity I could do alone and be in full control. It also got me into an environment where I could be around other people, yet did not need to socialize if I did not feel well enough. It is well known that swimming is one of the best forms of exercise and stress reduction for people of all ages and life challenges (Katz, 1993). A good vigorous swim increases the oxygen in the blood that is delivered to the brain and also helps release endorphins into the blood. I found that I felt a meditative rhythm when engaged in swimming. The aerobic aspects of swimming pump the blood, which can help the heart and relax muscles. I found swimming to be a relatively inexpensive activity that significantly helped (and still helps) me deal with stress and promote my creative thinking patterns.

Swimming has helped relieve serious bouts of depression and helped with clearing my thinking patterns. Many times I have to push myself to get to the pool. Once I complete a 30- or 40-minute swim routine followed by a visit to a steam room, I find myself thinking much clearer, less anxious and more relaxed.

Pursuing further education and working also have been very important tools. Work validated my abilities and, fortunately, led to a good track record in competitive employment. In my recovery, I have needed a great deal of support and help to create the type of daily routine, such as setting a daily maintenance plan (Copeland, 1997) that supports recovery. Patience and persistence are the keys. I had to be patient with myself and others and persist even when I did not feel well. Early on I realized that if

> When I stopped blaming others and life's situations for the challenges imposed by my illness...I was more able to handle stress, disappointments, and even my successes.

I showed up, I would be rewarded. This is how my work ethic developed. I realized that I could go to work and contribute something, even though I was not fully well.

Accepting the illness and the related challenges is also key. When I stopped blaming others and life's situations for the challenges imposed by my illness, I perceived life as less stressful, and I was more able to handle stress, disappointments, and even my successes. Learning more about the illness and how I could be well despite my diagnosis was a relief. Working helped me get out of myself and continues to help me to overcome my obsessions and rituals. I have developed an attitude of acceptance and continue to learn new skills and access supports that keep me focused on daily goals. There is hope for everyone, and we need to be open to support one another.

It is my hope the mental health system, professionals, consumers, and families can work collaboratively to become self-empowered and self-directed to move beyond the label and think about the wellness within and around them. It is up to each one of us to assume our respective roles and responsibilities on a personal, professional, and system level to chart a course toward transforming the mental health system and our society, such that we can achieve a collective focus on recovery and wellness. The wellness approach offers a holistic framework in which to view the person as a whole being (physical, spiritual, emotional, environment, social, occupational-leisure, intellectual, and environmental dimensions). This framework is useful for consumers, professionals, and families to take control of their lives and capitalize on strengths, abilities, and personal aspirations in order for every individual to take on and fulfill meaningful roles within their families and in today's society.

References

Anthony, W. (1991). Recovery from mental illness: The new vision of service researchers. *Innovation and Research,* 1(1), 13–14.

Anthony, W. (1993). Recovery from mental illness: The guiding vision of the mental health service system in the 1990s. *Psychosocial Rehabilitation Journal,* 16(4), 11–23.

Anthony, W. (2000). A recovery oriented system: Setting some system level standards. *Psychiatric Rehabilitation Journal,* 24(2), 159–168.

Copeland, M. E. (2002). *Wellness Recovery Action Plan.* West Dummerston, VT: Peach Press.

Copeland, M. E., & Mead, S. (2004). *Wellness Recovery Action Plan & Peer Support: Personal, Group and Program Development.* West Dummerston, VT: Peach Press.

Deegan, P. (April 1988). Recovering: The lived experience of rehabilitation. *Psychosocial Nursing and Mental Health Services,* 31(4), 7–11.

Hutchinson, D. S. (1996) Promoting wellness in rehabilitation and recovery: A call to action. *Community Support Network News,* 11(2).

Johnson, J. (1986). *Wellness: A context for living.* Thorofare, NJ: Slack.

Katz, J. (1993). *Swimming for total fitness.* Broadway Books, NY.

Moller, M. D., and Murphy, M. F. (1997) The three r's: Psychiatric rehabilitation wellness program. *Psychiatric Rehabilitation Journal,* 20(3): 42–48.

Swarbrick, M., & Burkhardt, A. (2000). The spiritual domain of health. *Mental Health Special Interest Section Quarterly,* 23, 1–3.

Swarbrick, M. (1997, March). A wellness model for clients. *Mental Health Special Interest Section Quarterly,* 20, 1–4.

Weed, D. (1999). *Health lifestyle workbook for consumers of mental health services.* Fall River Health and Human Services Coalition, Inc., Massachusetts Health Research Institute.

My Journey of Spirituality and Resilience

Leonard Mulcahy

In 1988, I started to write in a journal to explore my experience with prayer and spirituality, my psychiatric illness, and my troubles. To this day, I still write and pray, but the words on the paper are different because I am viewing my illness in a different light. For these many years, my journal has been private, but now I am sharing my story with you. I hope that you will find this writing interesting and inspiring.

With time, I have come to consider that difficulties can teach us many different lessons. Our experiences can help us to better understand ourselves so that we may find out who we are and who we have become. After living with a psychiatric illness for the last 17 years, I feel that I now know who I am, where I am going, and who I have become. Isn't this what life is all about, to know oneself?

During this long journey, spirituality has given me the resilience and the capacity to bear and live with personal pain, to accept difficulties, and to find meaning in my experiences. Prayer has led me to this acceptance in my life, and there is not a day that goes by without prayer and a strong spiritual connection with God.

I grew up in a loving family with parents who demonstrated kind, considerate, and respectful values. My life with my brother, Neil, and sister, Lisa, was special and extremely happy. My parents and siblings always knew what was going on, and we stuck by each other's side. We attended church regularly, and our Catholic faith was important in those early years. As a child, I was innocent, healthy, and full of hope and love. My high school years were pleasant with a large group of friends and playing sports alongside my brother. My mental health was something I never thought about. I was always smiling and motivated to make new friends and curious about the new world around me.

In 1983, I entered the University of Massachusetts in Boston, which was my first choice as I wanted to attend a school close to home. I was motivated to get good grades and graduate. I thought that with hard work I could be a successful student and make a difference in society. I always had wanted to help people, so majoring in psychology seemed like a good idea. There was something about the human spirit that captured my heart, and I wanted to know how other people coped with and managed difficulties. I had no idea that I, myself, would need to develop resilience and coping skills later in life.

In college, I began to experience loneliness and the dark feeling of depression. I could not understand

> After living with a psychiatric illness for the last 17 years, I feel that I now know who I am, where I am going, and who I have become. Isn't this what life is all about, to know oneself?

This article was published in the *Psychiatric Rehabilitation Journal*, 2007, 30(4), 311–312, and is reprinted with permission.

what was happening because up until that point in my life, things had always gone well for me. During this time, I began to attend Mass in the school chapel looking for relief from the dreadful pain that was so difficult for me. Loneliness is the absence of having a connection to this world as a human being. I longed for connection and thought if I could just develop my social skills, I would make friends and feel better about myself. I was unaware that my loneliness was a result of my depression.

Resilience was a term I was not familiar with, but as my illness progressed, it became clear to me that I needed to be resilient in order to stay alive. I took a lot of time to pray, and my spiritual life became special to me as I was more able to feel a tender spiritual bond.

After college, I began to experience more painful and troubling thoughts and emotions. My symptoms included depression, paranoia, scrambled, and even suicidal thoughts. Being psychotic brought me into a world far away from the world that I once knew. I believed that people were talking and laughing about me and as a result, I became more isolated and emotionless.

During this time, I turned to prayer and believed in the spiritual power of prayer for myself and for others. I prayed for people in need and for people who were on the street and homeless. Prayer was my life saver and helped me to find a place for myself in this world. Mother Teresa's words convey the meaning of prayer....

> Prayer is joy
> Prayer is love
> Prayer is peace
> You cannot explain it
> You must experience prayer
> It is not impossible
> God gives it for the asking

People also came into my life to help me to begin to manage my illness. I met a psychiatrist and a therapist who were both there for me during the most difficult times. When I felt sick and symptomatic, my therapist would ask me how my prayer life was going, and I would tell her that I was too sick to pray. She would encourage me to not give up hope on my spiritual strength and to believe in what gave me the will to live.

My horrible psychiatric symptoms never went away completely, but I felt less alone. Prayer helped me to love myself and to know that I am precious. Feeling valued and loved gave me strength even though days were difficult.

I also realized that part of being resilient is being involved with others. Right now, I am an active member of my parish and attend prayer groups weekly. I

I understand that loving myself is vital for survival.

volunteer in a soup kitchen and attend Mass weekly. Spirituality has given me unlimited strength during my journey with mental illness. I try not to focus on my illness, but instead I think about myself as a person who has a purpose in life: to serve as a child of God. My spiritual life provides support to assess my values and to treat people with respect, compassion, and loving kindness. Having a spiritual life allows me to have peace, love and joy in my heart, however lonely it is.

I understand that loving myself is vital for survival. When I experience love in my heart, I rarely feel unworthy, unloved, or misunderstood. When I sit in the chapel at my parish, I can let go of all my fears of pain and rejection.

Do I reject myself because I often have strange and painful emotions, or do I accept myself as I am? If I can't accept the pain that I harbor, then I pray for support and a spiritual acceptance of my suffering no matter how I feel.

Along my journey, which has been filled with many trials and tribulations, prayer has kept me moving forward down the right road of spiritual wholeness, instead of self-destruction and death. I am proud to be a Christian and a man of love and prayer, even when I am not feeling connected to the world or other people. When I pray, I can focus on being a child of God and not someone with a mental illness. Prayer allows me to be fully alive and spiritually awakened, which has made all the difference.

CHAPTER 4

Enhancing Personal Meaning

The Spiritual Meaning of Psychosis

Marcia A. Murphy

Psychosis can have profound meaning for persons who have experienced it. The meaning attached to psychotic episodes often can be found in the hallucinogenic content of the experience. This article describes themes that emerged from interviews I conducted with eight persons with psychiatric disabilities. I am also a psychiatrically disabled person, but this study focused on the experiences of others, some of whom attend a psychosocial rehabilitation center for people with mental illnesses, called a clubhouse. It is important for those involved with people with mental illnesses, i.e., the psychiatric community, to consider these themes. They call attention to painful struggles that may occur within the ill person's mind, often involving conflict between life and death. They point to attitudes, behaviors and beliefs that significantly influence the quality of life for those with psychiatric disabilities. Also, they show that, despite the suffering that psychoses cause, meaning may be found that promotes the sanctity of life. These themes have implications both for individuals who experience psychoses and for psychiatric professionals who treat them.

The terms *psychosis, hallucination,* and *mental illness* are derived from the medical model of disease common to mainstream psychiatry. Other models, based on diverse philosophies and world views, attribute psychiatric symptoms to varied origins, some of them supernatural or spiritual. Different models of health and disease do not necessarily invalidate one another, but may focus upon different aspects of an experience (Tamm, 1993). It is beyond the scope of this paper to evaluate different models along with their diverse labeling of mental phenomenon. Instead, I have chosen to use medical terms common to the Western psychiatric community, but the reader should be mindful that other interpretations of psychiatric illness exist. However, this paper's assertion is true regardless of which model is applied. For what I identified as "illness" is actually purposeful in nature and the success or failure of the "psychosis" has to do with universal truths regardless of the therapist's interpretation.

The psychosis—its experiential reality—has proven to have consequences in the daily life of the ill. For example, when voices call a person derogatory names, he or she feels persecuted and oppressed. Voices that threaten cause fear. And when they say, "Kill yourself!" some people follow their command and commit suicide. This means that hallucinations can be persuasive and cause intense emotional reactions that even may result in destruction of life. Therefore, it is wise for psychiatrists, therapists, and counselors to consider the content of hallucinations.

Over the years, I have seen heroic efforts made by psychiatric professionals to prevent clubhouse members from committing suicide. A feeling of despair overtakes many people with mental illnesses causing them to become suicidal. Often death romances them, making darkness look appealing. It seduces some into self-destructive behaviors through a gradual process,

This article was published in the *Psychiatric Rehabilitation Journal,* 2000, 24(2), 179–183, and is reprinted with permission.

such as smoking or an abrupt, violent end as in jumping off a tall building. Therefore, whatever gives hope and light to such people is valuable.

In the process of finding members of the clubhouse to interview for this study, I extended an invitation to anyone who had experienced a psychotic episode. No potential participant was excluded on account of his or her belief system or lifestyle. The age at which the eight persons interviewed had their first psychotic episode varied from seven years of age to thirty-five. The educational level completed was: three high school graduates, two with one or more years of college, one college graduate, and two with Master's degrees. There was no relationship between age of onset of hallucinations or educational level and the content of hallucinations. Even though some had experienced delusions, this study's primary focus was on hallucinations. The diagnostic break-down of participants was: six with schizophrenia, one with schizo affective disorder and one with bipolar disorder.

I asked participants about both negative and positive experiences. Some of both were reported. However, most participants emphasized an evil presence during their psychotic episode, while many reported good afterwards.

Nature of Psychoses

Beth was in college when she started to withdraw socially and then was hospitalized with her first psychotic episode. She heard frightening voices and felt like she was battling evil. It felt to her as though she were fighting for her life and the lives of her family and friends. She was terrified because she felt as though dark forces were trying to destroy her. She remembers that once, when locked in a quiet room, she kept looking for a crucifix. "I needed to see one," she said, "because I was fighting for my life."

Beth also remembers voices saying, "Kill your mother!" Other times they made racist remarks and called people derogatory names. They told Beth she was stupid and no good. The voices used profanity, cursing God, Jesus and the Holy Spirit. Beth believes her psychosis represented covert warfare.

When Janet first became ill, she heard six different voices. One said it was going to kill her. Another told her to kill the mayor, and the rest said a variety of things. At the time, she was attending seminary where the voices helped her write papers. When she received failing grades, she rewrote them without using the voices' suggestions. Occasionally, a voice said something positive like, "I love you." Janet said that, for her, the voices were real. From her religious background, she knew about Satan and believed they came from him. Janet felt a lot of fear during this time; she thought she was lost to Satan.

> Hallucinations can be persuasive and cause intense emotional reactions....it is wise for psychiatrists, therapists, and counselors to consider the content of hallucinations.

Ron was in a psychiatric hospital suffering from depression when he first became psychotic. He was on a low dose of an antidepressant when, suddenly, the staff increased it by four times the original amount. He said this triggered a psychotic episode. Not only did he hear voices—he had visual hallucinations. These were of rough looking men who motioned for him to come, then shook angry fists as though they were going to beat him up. He also had vivid nightmares. One time, the voices convinced him that he had killed his brother, which was untrue. He said they sounded malevolent, and he felt as though he were in hell.

Linda was only seven years old when she first heard voices. She experienced much abuse as a child. Contributing to the trauma that took place in her home were auditory hallucinations—voices that told her she was a bad person. Many times the voices told her to kill herself, that she would feel better if she died. They were persistent and became more malicious in her teen years when she began using street drugs and alcohol. The voices' strongest message was that, if she committed suicide, she would know God, heaven, and the spirit world. Then, she would come back to life. It told her that if she died, she would learn all the answers and be resurrected. Then, her life would be grand. As a result, she almost drank Drano. A counselor helped her get to a hospital before she hurt herself. Only a few times did a voice say something positive, such as, "Life is ok; you're doing ok."

Anne started having psychiatric problems in her thirties after giving birth to her fourth child. She heard voices for about twenty-four hours. One was the voice of a psychiatrist she had seen in the past. He was saying positive things about her to other people. She also heard imaginary airplanes flying over the house and music that changed quickly to match the mood and content of her thoughts. Anne did not report sinister hallucinogenic content; however, she was paranoid during her psychotic episode and believed her phone, house, and car were bugged.

Among the eight participants, Sue was unique because, when she was psychotic, she hallucinated in all five senses. She identified themes of good and evil. Some of the hallucinations were positive and uplifting, but the majority were negative. When psychotic, she thought there was an evil plot against her and her family. She felt pressure to do or say the right thing and felt that, if she made the slightest mistake, evil people or forces would kill her family as well as her. She was extremely frightened. When Sue was hospitalized, she was afraid to sleep at night for fear someone was going to kill her. At that time, many of the visual hallucinations were of small men that looked oriental. She felt they were wicked people.

She also felt there were levels of evil. There seemed to be a malicious presence and something similar to a pattern or maze. In her words, "There was a complicated entanglement that led to another even more evil level. And then this whole pattern would continue, it would go to one more level and one more level. I think there were only about four levels. But they were extremely scary. Each level was worse and more evil."

Barb was fourteen when she began to hear voices. As she described it, she began to talk to spirits. This frightened her. Also, once, when psychotic, her perception seemed surreal and she wanted to "scratch off her face."

Hannah was also fourteen when she began to hear voices, and they filled her with fear. They said they were going to "get her." She heard strange "talking in her head," and these inner voices often gave her false information. For example, they said that if she did not smoke a cigarette, something bad would happen to her. They called her derogatory names and told her she was a bad person. On one occasion, she thought satanic people were at the door of her room.

Strategies for Survival

From these examples, it is apparent that psychotic episodes can cause great suffering. The participants felt that dark, sinister forces were at work—sometimes aimed at destroying them and/or their loved ones. Many believed the voices were real. But, real or imagined, their influence was felt. And, to propound their misery, many had existential crises following their psychotic episodes. They questioned whether there was any meaning in life or purpose to their existence. Such questioning sometimes caused depression, but the participants' religious faith or personal spiritual conviction often provided answers. Some became involved in organized religious communities, while other kept to private, individualized spiritual beliefs and practices.

Some participants found in their belief systems a source of strength to counter dark forces. Their religious faith and practice also fostered attitudes that promoted health and well-being. Such faith may contribute toward progress in psychiatric treatment (Fallot, 1998; Sullivan, 1998). Psychiatric professionals—even those who lack religious perspective—need to be aware of this resource and listen to their client's religious experiences and concerns.

Regardless of a therapist's spiritual beliefs or lack of them, it is prudent for him or her to recognize attitudes and practices that increase mental stability and emotional well-being (Richards & Bergin, 1997). For several of those I interviewed, it was their faith in God that kept them from killing themselves. Just as the "evil forces" of psychosis had destructive consequences, good forces of religious beliefs—those that incorporated spiritual reality into personal experience— also had their consequences. By incorporating "spiritual reality into personal experience," I mean that the person came to view the world and reality with a spiritual perspective. Based on this perspective, they focused their attention on spiritual truths, some of which are found in scripture, and participated in activities, such as prayer or meditation that connects them to the spiritual source. Also, for those involved in organized religion, this included church activities. This spiritual awareness and participation empowered them to make positive changes in their lives. The resulting improvement in the participant's mental condition often was substantial and worthy of consideration.

> Some participants found in their belief systems a source of strength to counter dark forces. Their religious faith and practice also fostered attitudes that promoted health and well-being.

The implications are clear. Those who have suffered from, what was for them, evil oppression may find strength to carry on with their lives, often in very productive ways. For example, Beth said that her faith now gives her hope. She believes she survived because of her relationship with a higher power and because people prayed for her. Beth reads the Bible daily, prays, attends Bible study, and church services. She says it is important to be able to discuss her faith with her counselor because it is a big part of her life. It really matters to her.

Ron explained how his faith helped him to get through his psychosis. He says he now has a better attitude and feels better because Jesus is his Savior. He has hope for the future. Ron said religion does not come up much in conversations with psychiatric professionals. He said he has not mentioned his religious beliefs very often because he thinks many psychiatrists and therapists dismiss religious beliefs as delusions— which they are not. He wants to protect himself and keep his faith private. Up until the time of his psychotic episode, Ron had been an atheist. He became a Christian after his mental breakdown.

Linda has found that prayer helps her. In her words, "God gives me strength, gives me strength within myself to better myself. Prayer makes me stronger. I pray every morning." Reading the Bible increases her faith and the ability to cope. She said there are passages that apply to her situation, one being, "I can do everything through him who gives me strength." Php. 4:13 (New International Version). Linda believes God helped her get through the experience of delusions and hallucinations so that she might continue with life. She said that before turning to God she despaired; she didn't think there was anyone "out there" for her. She says that her faith and religious activity now give her hope.

Sue believes she would not have been able to survive without her faith. She says she would have killed herself. For the most part, her psychiatrists and therapists have been supportive of her relationship with the Lord and of her support system through the church. They have been very encouraging. For a while, she had a therapist who didn't believe in God but felt a spiritual connection through nature. But, Sue told her about her activities within the church and her religious perspective, and this therapist was supportive of that whole aspect of her life.

However, earlier, Sue had a therapist that didn't approve of her religious practice. This therapist was an atheist and felt that Sue's church, pastor, family, and religious friends had too much influence on her, and that her relationships with them were unhealthy. She thought Sue needed to distance herself from these people and rediscover who she was and what she wanted in life. So the therapist advised Sue to cut off her relationship with God, the church, and her family.

The therapist said she was taking Sue apart so as to put her back together and make her a new person.

> After going through all the struggles, trials, and tribulations of coping with a mental illness, I feel I am a better person than I might have been otherwise.

Sue said the therapist succeeded in taking her apart, but never put her back together. She said: "I was floundering and lost, and I got in with the wrong kind of people. I started drinking quite a bit, and that was the time I got hooked on smoking." Fortunately, after about six months, Sue started seeing a new therapist, and reestablished her relationship with God and her religious support network.

Sue believes in a holistic approach to mental health that includes the health of mind, spirit, and body. She also believes that a relationship with a higher power is important. She has found her faith compatible with ideas about recovery and mental health. For her, recovery in mental health terms is "living the most satisfying and fulfilling life possible despite having a mental illness."

Even though those who participated in this study saw their faith as important in their recovery, they also stressed the importance of medication. Their religious beliefs did not conflict with drug or psychological therapies.

Conclusion

The examples of psychosis given above had strong experiential themes. First of all, these psychotic individuals felt they were under demonic attack. Second, they felt they were bad people because of negative comments made about them. And third, they believed they were in a struggle to survive, to save their own lives or the lives of others. Less often, positive themes emerged, but this occurred infrequently. When hallucinations involved beautiful, encouraging, or supportive content, some found these to have real meaning and considered them to be divine in nature. Still, others believed them to be deceptions on the part of the devil.

When asked what impact psychosis had had and what meaning they had found in illness, more positive themes emerged. For example, Beth responded that her psychosis had made her stronger. She said she has had to fight and struggle for most of her life. But also, the illness has given her a different outlook from most people. She finds herself more accepting of those who are different because of their disabilities, illnesses, etc. She sticks up for people with disabilities when others discriminate against them.

When Sue was asked how her illness had affected her philosophy of life, she replied, "I feel I am a different person because I have had mental illness. It is difficult to say, but after going through all the struggles, trials, and

> With proper treatment and support, psychotic episodes have transformative potential (Grof, 1998).

tribulations of coping with a mental illness, I feel I am a better person than I might have been otherwise. I might have been more shallow and superficial. I think I'm more able to empathize with and help other people. And, with my current job, I find that I have an opportunity, as a mental health advocate, to help a lot of people, and that adds a great deal of meaning to my life."

As stated above, both Beth and Sue felt that psychiatric illness had changed their lives in positive ways. Therapy should involve exploration in depth for such beneficial and positive changes that may have taken place and provide encouragement for them to evolve. With proper treatment and support, psychotic episodes have transformative potential (Grof, 1998).

However, even with the positive life-changing qualities, mental illness can be devastating for those who experience it. It often takes months or even years to recover from a psychosis. The negative affects of a psychotic episode include depression and a loss of will to continue living. A relationship with a higher power may be the only safeguard against suicide. It is increasingly evident that, in conjunction with medication, a spiritual life aids people with mental illnesses. Thus, reliance on the psychiatric community is only one part of the equation, and when the psychiatric professional listens to the spiritual beliefs held by persons with psychiatric disabilities, this aids in the healing process (Richards & Bergin, 1997; Sullivan, 1998). Clients' interpretations of their psychotic episodes and how to deal with them have relevance. And, often the solutions they find give real meaning to their lives.

References

Fallot, R. D., (1998). The place of spirituality and religion in mental health services. *New Directions for Mental Health Services: Spirituality and Religion in Recovery from Mental Illness, 80,* 3–12.

Grof, Stanislav (1998). Human nature and the nature of reality: Conceptual challenges from consciousness research. *Journal of Psychoactive Drugs, 30*(4), 343–357.

Richards, P. S. & Bergin, A. E. (1997). A spiritual strategy for counseling and psychotherapy. Washington, D.C.: American Psychological Association.

Sullivan, W. P. (1998). Recoiling, regrouping, and recovering: First-person accounts of the role of spirituality in the course of serious mental illness. *New Directions for Mental Health Services: Spirituality and Religion in Recovery from Mental Illness, 80,* 25–33.

Tamm, M. E. (1993). Models of health and disease. British *Journal of Medical Psychology, 66,* 213–228.

I feel a kind of
harmony and
balance between
body, mind,
and spirit.

This is a favorite picture of mine. Words like peace, serenity, and tranquility come to mind when I look at this picture. I feel a kind of harmony and balance between body, mind, and spirit. This photograph represents peace of mind for me, which is a rarity these days. Nature is quite healing, unfortunately its amazing beauty often is lost to locked doors for those of us who suffer from mental illness. If we work together maybe, we can build a bridge and see our way to new forms of recovery. Recovery, that if you look long enough, will include moments like this one captured everyday all around us.

—LMV, from *Picturing My Health*, 2005

From Depths of Despair to Heights of Recovery

Holly Henderson

The definitions of recovery included in the NAMI (National Alliance for the Mentally Ill) *"Family-to-Family" Education Program* (second edition, 2001) capture the meaning of recovery as I myself have experienced it. I quote from the Program:

> Patricia Deegan, a consumer who is a clinical psychologist and a leader in the recovery movement, has written extensively on the meaning of recovery. In her words: "[Recovery is] a decision to meet the challenge of disability....People experience themselves as *recovering* a new sense of self and purpose within and beyond the limits of disability." This is something only the *self* can do; it is a decision to lead a hopeful life and to make a contribution in spite of the limitations imposed by illness.

> A further definition of recovery comes from Steven Kerkser, former head of the Florida Consumer Action Council: "Recovery is not remission, nor is it a return to a preexisting state. The idea that we can be 'cured' is counterproductive to recovery....

> Recovery is the development of new ego and identity structures to replace those damaged by our illnesses. Recovery is about wellness, that is, the redevelopment of a new and healthier personality and lifestyle, an independent personality that is strong enough to stand on its own. Recovery takes place through creation of new patterns of behavior that make our lives more satisfying and productive.

> People in recovery like themselves as they are, accept their disabilities, and enjoy the lives they have. Acceptance of one's disability can lead to greater appreciation of one's own strengths and new levels of self-esteem. Recovery is based on personal choice, responsibility, self-determination and self-esteem.

Full acceptance and realization of these truths came gradually for me and for many others, I'm sure. Before moving on, I want it to be clear I appreciate that some of us with mental illnesses have much rougher rows to hoe. For some, recovery perhaps will perhaps mean just learning to cope with the symptoms of their illnesses on a day-to-day basis. Their futures may seem to others as rather bleak. They may not realize employment, independent living, marriage, and families of their own, if desired, or other achievements and joys in life. But I believe life holds measures of purpose and happiness for everyone.

The road I've traveled on my way to recovery from serious mental illness is long, the journey often arduous. A client of the W. G. Nord Community Mental Health Center in Lorain, Ohio, since the age of 28, I am diagnosed as having schizoaffective bipolar mixed disorder as well as obsessive compulsive tendencies. Born in 1954, I believe I've suffered significantly from symptoms of these maladies since early childhood.

For me, having schizoaffective bipolar mixed disorder has meant, in part, experiencing episodic deep depression as well as periods of extreme elation, having seemingly boundless physical energy and feeling no limits to what I can accomplish—mania. Left unchecked, either of these emotional states can and

This article was published in the *Psychiatric Rehabilitation Journal,* 2004, 28(1), 83–87, and is reprinted with permission.

have led to psychosis, with symptoms indicative of impaired contact with reality.

Everyone has experienced periods of depression or elation in his/her life. The differences in my case are the causes—alterations in brain chemistry—along with the frequency, severity, and duration of such episodes. I sometimes experience both depressive and manic symptoms at the same time. It's as though I use manic symptoms to cope with an undercurrent of depression that sometimes breaks through to the surface.

Contributing to the depression is the fact I've lived my whole life feeling essentially emotionally isolated from others, like I haven't fit in or belonged. I've felt tolerated to some extent by those with whom I've shared some degree of distant friendship. To compensate, I daydream and fantasize a lot about the person I would like to be and the life I want to experience. From my earliest memories—but less so in recent times—I've lived in a fantasy world, sharing my life with fictional characters in fictionalized settings. My friends and foes have been characters I have borrowed from real life, books, and television, as well as others I've just made up. For them I have created in my mind living arrangements, vocations, and employment settings. I've shared a lot of mental conversation with them as well as mentally enjoyed social events with them. Sometimes, I've unwittingly expressed emotions by facial expressions that cause observers to wonder why or what I'm thinking about. So, while aware of my physical surroundings, I have been absorbed in my own mind and world a major part of the time. Mania either has fueled this or resulted from it, or both—I cannot say which it has been.

There are other symptoms and physical evidences of the manic and/or depressive ideation going on. I sometimes feel tremendous physical energy translated into very brisk walking or, if indoors, just jumping up and down in place for long periods of time, usually while listening to music. Depression can be paralyzing in that I sometimes cannot force myself to get out of bed. Sometimes sleeping too much, sometimes I experience long periods of insomnia. Sometimes experiencing loss of appetite, sometimes I'm insatiable. I may

neglect good personal hygiene. Lack of concentration, poor memory, racing thoughts, pacing the floor, bouts of crying or laughter, rapid speech, irritability or blatant anger, swearing, and spending sprees are symptomatic of my emotional turmoil, as well. I've threatened myself with suicidal ideation but only once seriously attempted it.

While I've experienced psychosis, it has not been in the usual sense of visual or auditory hallucinations. Rather, I may misinterpret what I actually do see or hear in my surrounding environment. For example, I once was hospitalized in late summer/early fall. One morning I looked out the window in my hospital room and saw a large white gas cylinder. I told myself that since this was a hospital it must contain oxygen, and oxygen tanks are green, so it must have snowed during the night. I didn't consider at that point that hospitals use other gases or that the "oxygen" tank was the only object snow covered, and way too early in the season, at that. I recall two psychotic delusions I experienced while in a manic episode. One was an unshakeable belief that God wanted me to be the national leader of women's ministries for the Assembly of God churches. The other was that God wanted me to enroll in a Bible college in preparation for becoming involved in urban Christian missionary work. Psychosis can be extremely frightening, such as paranoid feelings that others are discussing me, poking fun at me or out to get me, or do me physical harm. I sometimes confuse what I'm thinking with what others may say and conclude that people can read my mind. There are times when I experience feelings I believe akin to dissociation: "I

> Contributing to the depression is the fact I've lived my whole life feeling essentially emotionally isolated from others, like I haven't fit in or belonged.

look, but I do not see. I hear, but I do not listen. I touch, but I do not feel." (Author unknown.)

Despite all of this, for many years it was especially difficult for me to understand I suffered from mental illness. I readily acknowledged experiencing periods of depression, sometimes prolonged and severe. But I believed this was more or less true for everyone, and therefore, just a normal part of the human condition. As for mania, it felt wonderful to have such energy to pursue many projects and dream many dreams. Obsessive-compulsive tendencies have led me to strive unrealistically toward perfectionism in housekeeping, in education, on the job, etc. Realizing I sometimes drive myself too hard, I still find reaching for excellence, *in theory,* an admirable goal. I just have to remember not to overextend my reach.

I've had several hospitalizations over the years, but it wasn't until my most recent one, in May of 2001, that I realized the emotional ups and downs, and perfectionism, were not the norm for the majority of people. And that other people could observe my behavior as outside the norm, while I myself was caught up in it and lacked objectivity. When therapists listed symptoms of bipolar thinking and behavior on a chalkboard, for example, I finally saw myself in what they wrote. Accepting the diagnoses was the first step toward recovery.

But accepting the diagnoses was, for me, most difficult because I had to overcome my own stigma about being one of *them.* I wrongly had lumped together all people with mental illnesses and considered them to be lazy, immature, and/or stupid. I always had believed a mentally ill person, while maybe having problems, really needed most of all to just pull him or herself up by the bootstraps. Such thinking always had led me to dismiss any need for therapy and medication for myself.

Nevertheless, inexplicably, I never missed a scheduled therapy session without good reason. But I never really could engage in therapy, except to vent negative feelings about other people, most especially my parents. No, they weren't role models of good mental health themselves in some respects, but I now accept that they were doing the best they could do. With

maturity comes greater acceptance of self and others with their flaws as well as their strengths. I also was (and sometimes still am) leery of therapy because I feared sharing too much, at times, might result in my facing prolonged hospitalization (I've had some bad experiences at some hospitals). Or my having to take medications with annoying or serious side effects. Or my being kept from seeking employment—and I have a very strong work ethic.

> Accepting the diagnoses was, for me, most difficult because I had to overcome my own stigma about being one of *them.*

As for medication, I didn't need it; my problems were *functional,* not *organic*—organic meaning the result of a brain disorder. But I wasn't openly rebellious on this account. I made sure I refilled prescriptions on time in case my psychiatrist would ever check to see if I was taking them. When a laboratory test was scheduled to check on the levels of medication in my bloodstream, I made sure I took the medication a full week in advance. During the most recent hospitalization, I finally decided I would start taking medication faithfully to see if it would be of any help. This is because I was feeling hopeless, and sick and tired of being sick and tired. It took several months, but I did start feeling better and decided to just stay on the meds, once and for all. And I attribute one of the reasons I'm now feeling and doing well to this medication compliance I fought for so long.

Now accepting that I do indeed have an illness, I also respect the importance of recognizing symptoms. I'm now very aware that I cannot rely on purely subjective thoughts and feelings to determine the state of my mental health. I hope I will remain trusting of others to clue me in when I seem headed for problems.

During the hospitalization to which I've referred, recreation and occupational therapists introduced me to new leisure activities. I had never thought of doing arts and crafts projects, but now enjoy them very much. I enjoy language and am an avid reader, as well as interested in writing. Listening to music, as well as playing the keyboard, is uplifting and/or soothing, depending on how I feel at the time. These activities help me unwind and relax as well as build my self-esteem.

It probably wasn't until I reached my mid-twenties that my family became aware of the seriousness, or even existence, of my illness. It began to play havoc with my education and employment, at that point; this sometimes makes me very angry, if I dwell on it. I had to realize a change in my career goals. I hold a BS degree in biology and completed an additional two and a half years toward an MD degree. The stress of a medical education overwhelming me, I withdrew from medical school. Then began my ride on an employ-ment roller coaster. I've held many jobs (10 plus) lasting from several hours to several years. My favorites were working as a nurs-ing assistant, library associate, and pre-school teacher—

> My religious faith and local church are very important sources of meaning and purpose in my life.

jobs I managed to hold and do well at for at least a year or longer. I've sometimes had to accept jobs not commensurate with my abilities. Although I was never fired, I left jobs for reasons that never were, or are, clear to me. I know at times I felt threatened by my coworkers but could not explain at those times, or now, why. My family always has provided me with a home and the necessities of life, when their help was needed. However, they and I never openly broached the subject of mental illness and what was going on with me. The subject seemed taboo. Often, I felt they really didn't care to be around me and didn't value any input into their conversations that I may have had. I sometimes sensed they harbored embarrass-ment and hostility and felt exasperated with me. I felt blamed for the symptoms of my illness.

This has changed. They encouraged my most recent hospitalization, an obvious turning point in my recovery. The nature of the illness having been dis-closed, they've made efforts to educate themselves about it. They share with me relevant information they come across. I feel they want to be involved in my life and share more of their own lives with me. They acknowledge how well I'm handling my life and employment now, including just recently attending a dinner at the Nord Center honoring clients' efforts in obtaining and maintaining employment. I receive phone calls and invitations to visit in their homes and attend social activities with them. The family has always gathered together to share birthdays, holidays, graduations and other major events in our lives. Although I'm a quiet person by nature, I sense their interest in including me more in conversation. If I need advice or help with household or car repairs, they are very willing to help out. More so than ever, I sense we are a family and "there for each other."

My religious faith and local church are very important sources of meaning and purpose in my life. I pick up a lot of philosophy and psychology from the Bible and in sermon texts. Studying and meditating on Biblical teachings, along with prayers and worship offered to my God, allow me to understand, accept, and forgive myself and others—just as God forgives me; to just "vent" sometimes; and demonstrate for me hope in any situation by recounting the sufferings of Biblical characters and how they overcame them. I'm working consciously on building relationships in women's groups that offer friendship and support to each other, in addition to sharing their faith.

I want to concentrate now on the importance of employment in my recovery. In the past, clients with serious mental illnesses were told they probably could not or would not be able to work again. I was told this and it was devastating—and also has been proven to have been wrong. Also in the past, psychotropic drugs—those used to treat brain disorders—were not as effective as the newer ones on the market today. These newer drugs have fewer disconcerting side effects. Medication and therapy have made it possible for me and for many others to enjoy successful employment. Now the best indicator that one can work is that he or she wants to work. And one does not have to be completely symptom-free, but rather, able to adapt when it's at all possible. One therapist related an instance when an employed client told her one day he could work no longer. He was Jesus Christ, you understand, and created the world—enough work for anyone. The therapist told him that even if it were true, he still needed to go to work that day and better hurry so he wouldn't be late.

Employment is the difference between thriving and just surviving. Along with my disability income through Social Security and Medicaid coverage, it provides me relative financial security. A single person not working is very likely to be living below the poverty level, able to do little more than pay his/her bills. This is scary. Working may allow one to live on his/her own, although group homes and government-subsidized housing are always possibilities for the unemployed disabled. As income increases, discretionary funds become available, allowing one to enjoy leisure activities.

Working decreases feelings of social isolation—staying at home with perhaps little to do but sleep, eat, watch television, and ruminate over problems, or worse, becoming involved in substance abuse, as sometimes happens. It puts in perspective personal problems, as one becomes aware of the difficulties others face, while still coping with the activities of daily living.

Employment has greatly increased my self-esteem and given me greater overall independence. Since October of 2001, I've been enjoying part-time employment doing clerical work for the Nord Center. Through the Nord Center, I have opportunities to speak to community and clients' groups sharing my story. Having completed the necessary training, I teach several different series of NAMI classes for recipients of mental health services and/or their families or significant others. I am a certified adult literacy tutor. Involved in the development of a "recovery center"—Gathering Hope House—for the mentally ill in Lorain County, I serve as acting president of its board of directors. I'm taking responsibility for myself, setting goals, and challenging myself to do more, taking risks. I feel like a "real person," taking on the responsibilities of adulthood.

There were things I had to do to make certain my success in these activities. I established routines for ensuring good nutrition (three squares a day), adequate sleep, regular exercise, continued compliance with taking medication, and keeping therapy appointments. My increased socializing helped me feel more comfortable around people. In preparation for writing resumes and filling out job applications, I collected information relevant to my work history. I considered the appropriateness of my wardrobe for interviewing and the kinds of work I like to do. And the Nord Center helped.

At the Nord Center, clients have one-stop service for a variety of mental health and related needs. Because all the service providers are under one roof, they hold each other accountable for the provision of quality care. I want to focus on the employment-related services. Clients may receive services for emotional and/or physical disabilities. The impact of working on income, such as disability and Medicaid benefits, actually is calculated by a benefits analysis counselor. There is vocational assessment to determine interests and suitability for various types of work.

> Employment is the difference between thriving and just surviving.

Arrangements can be made for trial work experience out in the community, which often results in offers of permanent employment. At the Nord Center itself, training is provided for those interested in maintenance work, clerical/computer positions, and for those interested in working in a commercial kitchen. Provision is made for gaining job-hunting skills, including resume writing and filling out job applications, as well as participation in mock interviews. Job leads are made available. Upon employment, an on-the-job coach is available, if needed, as well as other follow-up services to increase the likelihood of retaining employment. A rehabilitation services liaison interfacing with community employers and providing employee assistance is also an option.

There is a normal anxiety or fear accompanying a new job, for anyone, whether or not he/she suffers a mental illness. This is magnified for one who has a spotty work history or who is reentering the work force following a long period of unemployment, as those with mental illnesses often are. This can present problems at the job interview, which is stressful enough in its own right. Professional rehabilitation services providers can help with these issues. For example, I was coached on presenting myself as having a medical condition now well managed with medication.

> **Mental illness throws some of us some curves in life that others haven't had to negotiate. I encourage any and everyone to look to the future and plan for it— set goals and *act on them*.**

One worries whether employers or others will notice side effects of medication or behavioral symptoms of his/her illness, which may return or worsen. What happens if these problems require one to take time off? Perhaps, if this should happen, one would feel comfortable sharing a little more about his/her circumstances with the employer, if the employee has proven him/herself to be reliable. Employers need to know an employee will show up and that the employee's job is getting done. Sometimes a leave of absence can be accommodated, sometimes not, if the job has to be done and no one else is available to cover. Again, a rehabilitation specialist and/or human resources professional can help with these and other concerns one may have about getting into the job market. And don't forget the "Americans with Disabilities Act" has employee assistance as one of its goals.

I'm so grateful many financial and other barriers to mental health services are eliminated through programs supported by the general public and through generous private donations of money and volunteer services. In my case, I've benefited from the local community mental health center and community hospitals, NAMI, the Ohio Rehabilitation Services Commission, the Social Security Administration, and assistance from Medicaid, and the Food Stamps programs. These services along with my family and friends provide me with a safety net that has enabled my recovery.

In conclusion, I emphasize that recovery is an *ongoing process*—not an end point one finally reaches. One learns the necessity of playing the cards he/she is dealt in life. But isn't this true of *living—for anyone?* It's just that mental illness throws some of us some curves in life that others haven't had to negotiate. I encourage any and everyone to look to the future and plan for it—set goals and *act on them*. Otherwise it might be said one's goal is to have no goals. Looking backward gets one nowhere unless he/she wants to learn from it. One must give serious thought to what he/she wants out of life and define what recovery means for him/herself—and pursue it.

With increased
societal education
and acceptance, I
also can be a part
of a community
and life. I can
move forward.

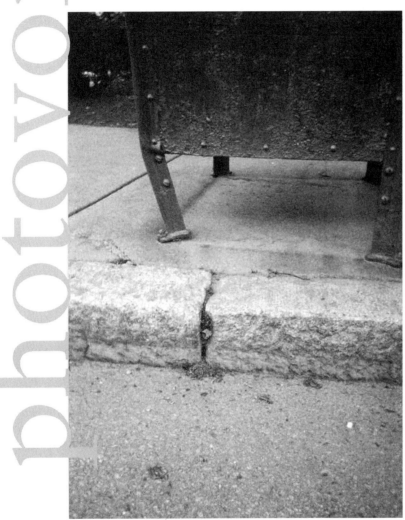

There is no message of strength or weakness or courage or cowardice here. Rather there is a mailbox. It sits with one leg that is bent. It is different. Yet it stands with the others. I am different. I am living with a mental illness. Yet, with increased societal education and acceptance, I also can be a part of a community and life. I can move forward.

—KMH, from *Picturing My Health,* 2005

Calculated Risk-Taking and Other
Recovery Processes for My Psychiatric Disability

Richard Weingarten

The first pillar in my recovery foundation came when my therapist, Aaron Lazare, MD, put me in the driver's seat in my efforts to recognize the problems I was experiencing. He helped me learn to monitor myself and my interactions with people, places, and situations that overwhelmed me or were problematic and to make notes and keep a journal of these experiences. Within a short time I could recognize the problems and evaluate them, discuss them coherently with my therapist, and progressively find ways to reduce or eliminate the distressful situations. What emerged from this effort was a three-step coping method: identifying, evaluation, and doing something to offset the problems.

Many years later John Strauss, MD, and a Yale researcher in a symposium on schizophrenia that I attended confirmed this method of coping. Strauss put different terms on a strategy that was "self-monitoring, self-evaluation, and self-action." This strategy was helpful with problems like sensory overload: in a busy restaurant, at a sporting event, inside a busy mall or at large family gatherings my senses would be overwhelmed and shut down. I had three choices. Let's say it's a busy restaurant at a peak hour: I could sit in a corner of the restaurant with my back to the room, leave the restaurant and go to another restaurant, or leave and come back at a less busy time.

Another application of this strategy helped me deal with mishaps, reversals, and setbacks in my life. Once a mishap or a mistake occurred, a critical inner voice would berate me in a punishing way and send me into a tailspin and often into depression. A few years after leaving treatment with Dr. Lazare, a psychiatrist warned me that I had to find a way of controlling this critical voice or it would destroy me. It took some effort to recognize the critical inner voice, which was my father's voice criticizing me, stop it and get my thoughts moving in a positive direction again.

> The first pillar in my recovery foundation came when my therapist...put me in the driver's seat in my efforts to recognize the problems I was experiencing.

There were a few strategies that I used that were of help: I could turn my attention to performing a simple task. I also could sit in a chair for 15 minutes and meditate on where the difficulty was coming from until it went away. Or I could lie down for 20 to 30 minutes until my mind and body were clear and quiet again. I continued to write about these distressing situations in my journal. This always helped to alleviate the distress and agitation. In general, I found that keeping a journal about my problems was one way for me to maintain a state of well-being. Consumers have told me that playing a musical instrument helped them "see" where they were emo-

This article was published in the *Psychiatric Rehabilitation Journal*, 2005, 29(1), 77–80, and is reprinted with permission.

tionally or engage in some other activity, like writing poetry, cooking, or working out.

The next pillar in my recovery was discovering the benefits of reasonable risk-taking. I was a nervy, risk-taking child and my family encouraged this bent. Joining the Peace Corps after college was a big risk, but reasonable for me, especially when the Peace Corps posted me in a small town in the interior of Brazil where I had only the rudiments of Portuguese, the Brazilian language. That turned out to be one of the best experiences of my life, and it was full of risk-taking.

And it was an even more risky venture that turned out to be key to a major breakthrough. It was two years into my recovery, and I missed Brazil and the part of myself that I found there. I approached the director of John Carroll University's Continuing Education program about teaching a class in Portuguese. At the time I was depressed, but it was August, and the academic year was about to start and I had to act if I wanted to teach the fall semester. I had researched the availability of Portuguese classes in colleges and universities in the Cleveland area and found that none of these institutions were offering Portuguese. I took this information to the Continuing Education program, and the director struck a deal with me. If I could recruit ten people for the class, she would run it. I put up notices advertising the class at the coffeehouses and bookstores near the university and contacted the corporations that had subsidiaries in Brazil. I even advertised at the Cleveland Clinic because I knew that wealthy Brazilians went there for their coronary problems. As it turned out, two nurses from the Clinic signed up for the class. Eventually, I found 17 people interested in learning Portuguese. That was a very important step and it was full of risk-taking.

The 2-hour-a-week class became the main focus and high point of my week. I learned from this experience that the reason I could take this risk was because of how much I enjoyed speaking Portuguese, and I could imagine a successful outcome. From my observations, I'm convinced that consumers don't appreciate how much they can do when they're symptomatic. Some consumers don't take risks because they can't

see themselves succeeding, especially if they are depressed. Risks, such as going on new medication, going off old medications, and going back into the community after lengthy hospitalizations often are

> Within a short time I could recognize the problems and evaluate them, discuss them coherently with my therapist, and progressively find ways to reduce or eliminate the distressful situations.

often not seen as the risks they are. People working with consumers can help them recognize the risks they take every day and the courage they show. In my case, I had a dysthymia condition that went untreated for 19 years and was mildly depressed every few days. But I managed to hold down many part-time and full-time jobs. I knew I wasn't functioning at my best, but I pushed through the depression and anxiety and proved to myself that I could be effective even when I was less than 100%. This was an important step and it was risky.

Now for the last ten years, I have worked as director of Consumer Initiatives and Education at the Connecticut Mental Health Center in New Haven. In this position, risk-taking continues to play a major role in starting new programs for consumers and people in recovery from addictive disorders. Understanding the importance of succeeding in a risk-taking venture, I've limited the risks to ensure the consumers and people in recovery succeed. In one program I founded, "The Recovery is for Everyone (RIFE)" Consumer Grants Program, I was able to help other consumers take risks. I know the benefits of creating projects and how these projects give consumers something meaningful and constructive to do, how they can move people ahead in recovery, and involve them in the mainstream community. I know how stuck consumers can get as a result of the illness, stigma, and poverty because I had been stuck myself. I thought many consumers would jump at the chance to create a project that would fulfill some aspiration and move them ahead in their lives. At least the more adventuresome would get involved, I figured.

After my Consumer Initiatives Committee developed the RFP (Request for Proposal) and put it out, I went to all the consumer clubhouses in south central Connecticut and talked up the RIFE grants program. I offered to provide technical assistance for people filling out the RFP for grants up to $5,000. We had funding from the Department of Mental Health and Addiction Services (DMHAS) and the Women's Consortium of Connecticut. I asked all the groups I spoke to how many people would create a project and submit a proposal. At every clubhouse, a few people raised their hands in affirmation. I was encouraged. The first year we got back 37 proposals and 26 were funded. Of these, 25 were taken to completion!

> The next pillar in my recovery was discovering the benefits of reasonable risk-taking.

One individual wanted to become a disc jockey, and he received funding for the purchase of mixers/ scratchers, speakers, and training from a well-known local disc jockey. Another grant recipient gave tap dance instruction to inner city children. A pair of people who had previously been homeless did a gardening project to market vegetables and flowers locally. Last year, in the fourth grant cycle of this program, 158 proposals were turned in and 61 were funded! Sixty of the 61 funded projects were brought to completion! In the first year of the RIFE program awards were given in the following areas: 32% business startups, 20% educational or vocational training, 16% peer support groups, 16% arts, 12% psycho-educational, and 8% health promotion or physical fitness

(Tracy, Weingarten, Mattison et al, 2004). We learned how successful consumers can be when they engage in risk-taking projects and have a support structure of opportunity, resources, encouragement, technical assistance, and the successful examples of other consumers.

The third and final pillar of my recovery was discovering how to summon my own personal strengths and resources to go back and reclaim my personal voice and keep my place at the table in order to be successful in social activities, like professional meetings and social gatherings. To be myself in these social functions involved risk-taking as well. Like many consumers, I became withdrawn and reclusive during the years of my illness. I had to relearn social skills that I had allowed to atrophy.

Luckily for me, a friend began taking me to Sunday services at the Unitarian Society of Cleveland. The Society had a very active welcoming policy for visitors and new members, including consumers, and then the Worship Committee invited three of us consumers to tell our stories. This was risky, however surprisingly, this service turned out to be a godsend. After the service, the whole congregation lined up to shake our hands, introduce themselves, and tell us how much they appreciated our sharing our stories. The tremendous feedback gave me a sense of acceptance that was very uplifting. The Society also sponsored various committees, and I got on the Social Action Committee and helped host political refugees from Central America who were immigrating to Canada and spending the winter in Cleveland. The Society became a safe haven where I regained my social skills and made new friends.

Several years later, I recalled how helpful the Unitarian Society had been to me and other consumers, and I built a bridge connecting a Congregational Church and the Welcome Basket outreach program that I co-founded and directed in New Haven. The church became our home one day each week and provided us with a meeting room, a kitchen, and a VCR and monitor for movies. The Church's Trustees served us a sit-down lunch and got to know us. After a few weeks, they invited us to their Sunday service. Later, church members provided transportation to and from services for the consumers in our program. The minister also took an interest in us and led discussions on spirituality.

Based on these experiences, I believe faith-based communities have an important role to play in helping consumers regain social skills and reintegrate back into society. Also, church committees and activities give consumers valued social roles and meaningful activity.

> The third and final pillar of my recovery was discovering how to summon my own personal strengths and resources to go back and reclaim my personal voice and keep my place at the table in order to be successful in social activities, like professional meetings and social gatherings.

Participating in professional meetings at work posed a challenge for me because of my trauma history. Sitting around a table with people who have strong personalities (I work at Yale) was very difficult. But I kept going back, and gradually my confidence and desire to speak increased as I became familiar with the members of the committees and the procedures they were using. In the last couple of years, I've spoken at various center-wide meetings and programs and have begun to take a leadership role at the Center.

I believe serving on committees and boards can be a reintegrating experience for people in recovery, but certain steps must be taken to ensure the consumer's success. Consumers should not be tokens on committees. They should have at least one sympathetic and supportive non-consumer at the meetings. The mission or purpose of the committee or board, as well as its procedures and specialized language, should be spelled out before the consumers go to the first meeting. It helps if the role of the consumer, i.e. the consumer perspective, is clearly defined for the consumer and non-consumer members. If these measures aren't taken, consumer efficacy and satisfaction will flag and the consumer will be left feeling disgruntled and defeated.

The three processes of recovery described here—the three-step coping strategy, calculated risk-taking, and overcoming a personal trauma history—helped me to cope with and overcome many of the problems I associated with my illness and disability. Using these strategies and working hard every day I've found is rewarded with new skills, including discipline, greater self-confidence and self-esteem, better social interactions, job satisfaction, and the joy of self-fulfillment. But all this took effort and my own desire to reclaim my life. It took courage and the support from my supervisors, therapists, colleagues, and friends. I view these processes I've described in this article as being the foundation for developing a satisfying life.

It's best to conclude this article by citing Esso Leete, a consumer spokesperson, who once wrote that consumer/survivors were among the most courageous people that she knew. I agree.

References

Davidson, L., (2003). *Living outside mental illness: Qualitative studies of recovery in schizophrenia*. New York and London: New York University Press.

Tracy, K., Weingarten, R., Piselli, A. & Roundsaville, B. (2004). Moving beyond illness to recovery: The recovery is for everyone (RIFE) grants program. *Psychiatric Rehabilitation Journal, 28*(2), 129–135.

photovoice

At that moment,
I feel well
and powerful
enough to handle
anything.

This is the path I ride my bike on. When I ride my bike, it helps me not only physically but emotionally. It helps clear my mind, give me an energy boost, and improves my mood. When I'm riding, it's like I'm in the middle of a big and busy world, but yet I feel free and peaceful. At that moment, I feel well and powerful enough to handle anything. Sometimes people with mental illness get caught in the dreaded "inner world" and forget these activities can help them feel better. Professionals and anyone who is involved in supporting someone in recovery should encourage people to use these simple, alternative tools because sometimes they can work better—than medication.

—Karen, from *Picturing My Health*, 2005

Working with Schizophrenia:
Personal Insights Into Working with a Psychiatric Disability

Francis Gilfedder

Since the realization that paid employment was possible for a person with a psychiatric disability, my life has changed completely. In 5 years, I have moved from rehabilitation activity to volunteer work, then supported employment, and finally to my current job, a competitive employment position collecting data for psychiatric disability research. The development of routine, contact with supportive and encouraging people, a sense of progress in my skills and ability, and the knowledge that work can be deferred if illness emerges have improved my situation enormously, especially financially. This was possible because of people with enlightened attitudes and experience with schizophrenia and employment issues, and my own determination and struggle. I have been lucky that my skills, interests, and beliefs have led me to be accepted in my current workplace. Many people I know with a psychiatric disability have a hard time finding a workplace or even an effective rehabilitation service, with some exceptions (Deegan, 2003).

Before my first episode, most of my goals were geared around improving my musical career; money was not a big ambition. Many stressful factors and my genetic predisposition led to my first breakdown and eventual hospitalization at age 29 years.

While I was in hospital, a case worker asked me about employment, but I didn't know what he was talking about and didn't treat it seriously. After leaving the hospital in 1999, I became obsessed with karma, and saw working in my parents' garden as a way of accumulating good karma. A friend invited me to their permaculture farm at an alternative lifestyle community in the country. Although I was in a very confused state of mind, I stayed for 5 months and worked on the farm every day, starting with simple tasks like dishwashing, moving on to collecting firewood and maintaining the fire in winter, and eventually learning more developed permaculture gardening techniques, until work became a basic habit no matter how many delusions I experienced or how lost in my own head I was. Eventually my friend couldn't support me any longer, so I returned to the city. One day I saw a man with a physical disability in a Pizza Hut uniform on the bus, which gave me a great leap of hope that if he could get a job, why couldn't I?

I became aware through my support group of a psychosocial rehabilitation program based on the clubhouse model (Beard, Propst, & Malamud, 1982), and I joined. On the first day at the clubhouse, someone commended me on my good work, so I decided to come back. I kept coming back for 5 years, and had fun, made friends, and improved my confidence and work skills. The clubhouse was not always utopia,

> Since the realization that paid employment was possible for a person with a psychiatric disability, my life has changed completely.

This article was published in the *Psychiatric Rehabilitation Journal,* 2007, 31(2), 161–163, and is reprinted with permission.

but the staff always were encouraging and focused on work.

After 6 years of clubhouse activity, including Transitional Employment (TE) (Bilby, 1999), I discovered a research position advertised through the clubhouse. A support worker accompanied me to the interview, and the employer was someone I knew from conferences organized by the clubhouse. The clubhouse director gave me an excellent reference. I was very happy to be selected, even surprised.

I am currently employed on a contract basis conducting telephone survey research related to role functioning of people living with a psychiatric disability. My employer has extensive knowledge of employing people with schizophrenia, and I had no problem disclosing my disability.

The fact that the employment is in the field of mental health means that everyone on the job is educated to the issues involved in mental illness, which is a big help, but my employer informed me that I was chosen over applicants who did not have an illness and had better educational qualifications. Therefore, this position is competitive employment, not a sheltered one.

> Taking a step towards employment is courageous because there is always the risk of relapse and hospitalization.

I have contact with many people with psychiatric disabilities who seek competitive employment, and it is rare for them to find a job that meets their talents and skills exactly. Taking a step towards employment is courageous because there is always the risk of relapse and hospitalization. Fortunately, this has not happened to me.

Current Employment Issues

Motivation and skill improvement. I work long hours in the office alone and must motivate myself to keep the work and interest going. I have to maintain compassion and interest for the people I am interviewing; chatting and making the interviews personable is important. I also have to stay aware of accuracy by checking and rechecking the database. I get energy from co-workers when relating to them, as energy levels are a major issue in my schizophrenia management.

All the tasks I have been given are well within my ability and involve a lot of repetition, so I continue to improve. I never thought I had people skills, but I have learned. I have my own style of dealing with a diverse range of people, trying to create a natural atmosphere for conversation and not making the research too intimidating. If the person being interviewed is afraid of giving information over the phone, I tell them that the research we are doing is for the good of everyone accessing mental health services. If they are frightened of how the government might use the research, I assure them that people who have experienced psychosis never will be forced to work unless they wish to. If someone is being difficult or unpleasant (rarely happens), I continue the interview, engage less, and simply request the relevant information, or try another time. Many people find the interview an opportunity to talk about their condition or employment and rehabilitation issues, as they have not yet found a listening ear; and some ask for contacts or advice on how to access services. I direct them to the nearest disability employment services.

Support. I receive ongoing support from the clubhouse. I have a visit from staff at the clubhouse every two months; they can boost confidence and help with tasks that may be daunting. They helped organize the hard copies of the interviews, assisted with monitoring the first few interviews, and currently, we have lunches for moral support. I call the clubhouse to discuss issues.

Flexible hours. Flexibility can be excellent for a person working with schizophrenia; when I am not feeling up to it, I can postpone the work to when conditions are better. I work 20 hours a week over 4 days, with the hours flexible to suit research participants or to suit my work preference.

I also work another job doing musical performances, so when I have a performance I can make up the hours later. Music keeps me sane and improves life quality, not to mention paying well at times. Usually a performance includes two 50-minute shows at a school, with rest afterwards. I get lots of energy from my fellow musicians, and they have great faith in my ability.

Productivity and inspiration. I maintain a standard of productivity that keeps my employer satisfied, but I wonder about other workplaces that have high quotas for employee productivity. For me, continued interest from my employer in the work and its standard gives pride in the product, and the interesting nature of the work inspires hope in the outcomes. Not all jobs can provide this. The knowledge that the data I collect will be used to help people with a psychiatric disability as well as the temporary benefit of them getting a gift voucher, is a strong motivation for me, and organizing information and using databases is always interesting, as is the data itself.

> In many ways my life has improved since before I became ill; I now have a real network of genuinely supportive friends and family, and am valued for who I am and what I can contribute.

Employability. As far as research is concerned, the difference between other employees and me is that I have direct knowledge of psychiatric disability and everything involved with it as well as an awareness of the culture of people living with a psychiatric disability, receiving benefits, or working. This experience gives my research a certain amount of validity or "halo" and generally makes research participants more comfortable, although some people decline to be interviewed by someone who is not a professional figure.

Current goals. I hope to remain in this situation and continue to increase my standard of musical ability and skills as a researcher, maybe even support a family. I once was asked how many years I have lost to the illness. They meant how long was I out of work, but the fact is I never will be the same person I was before the illness struck, and I may take medication for the rest of my life, so the real answer is that the rest of my life was partly lost to mental illness. However, in many ways my life has improved since before I became ill; I now have a real network of genuinely supportive friends and family, and am valued for who I am and what I can contribute, not just for being a funny guy.

I went to a party recently and everyone I met asked, "What do you do?" I had my answer ready for them, "Oh, just a bit of research." Little did they realize what a miracle it was to be able to say this in response.

References

Beard, J. H., Propst, R. N., & Malamud, T. J. (1982). Fountain House Model of Psychiatric Rehabilitation. *Psychosocial Rehabilitation Journal* 5(1), 47–53.

Bilby, R. (1999). Transitional employment: The most supported of supported employments. *The Clubhouse Community Journal, 1,* 34–36.

Deegan, G. (2003). Discovering recovery. *Psychiatric Rehabilitation Journal, 26*(4), 368–376.

My Personal Story of Coping

Marjorie Jacobs

Mania

Inside our house
no one sleeps.
Mother sings falsetto
to the blaring radio,
talks to strangers
over the telephone,
changes her outfits every hour,
stamps up and down stairs
all night long.

We bury our heads under pillows,
try to disappear between sheets,
pray father will make her stop
but his shouting, his swearing
can't subdue her.
He dials 911.

Sirens and her screaming
police officers and her crying
handcuffed they haul
our mother
away.

My mother's mental health has impacted my life since I was a young child and given me the gift of resiliency. She was first hospitalized and diagnosed with bipolar disorder when I was five years old. Her illness continued throughout my childhood and into my teenage years and frequently included yearly hospitalizations. Growing up with a family member who experienced a serious mental illness, I feared that

revealing the truth of her illness would mean instant rejection by my friends, neighbors, and teachers. It was our family's "secret," although it is likely that everyone knew about my mother's illness.

Dealing with aspects of the stigma, shame, embarrassment, stress, and secrecy isolated my father, two sisters, and me. Over time, we became isolated from our extended family and our community. We didn't request or receive support and help from neighbors and relatives. In fact, outside of our home, we pretended that everything was fine, and we were leading a normal life just like everyone else.

Perhaps due to the stress we experienced, my two sisters each became depressed and my father became angry. None of us received any professional help or support from social workers, therapists, or doctors. I simply watched, tried to accept my mother's illness and find ways to deal with my suffering.

Looking back, I often reflect on how I was able to cope with this difficult family situation and the suffering that I witnessed and experienced first-hand. In reality, my mother's ill health and denial taught me the importance of taking care of my own health, learning to deal with stress, and the importance of connecting with others, both human and animals. As long as I can remember, I have exercised daily, maintained good nutrition and adequate sleep, enjoyed learning and studying, valued friendship, and spent time writing poetry and playing a musical instrument. Unlike my siblings, I also was able to express compassion for my mother. I understood that she was sick

This article was published in the *Psychiatric Rehabilitation Journal*, 2008, 32(2), 135–137, and is reprinted with permission.

Growing up with a family member who experienced a serious mental illness, I feared that revealing the truth of her illness would mean instant rejection by my friends, neighbors, and teachers.

and not in control. When I was visiting my mother in private and state hospitals, I was flooded with sadness and love. My heart was always wide open to my mother and all the patients with whom I would talk and play ping-pong while visiting her.

After finishing graduate school, I reached a turning point in my life in that I realized that I could respond to my heart, my values, and my desire to find meaningful work by becoming a teacher and writer. Teaching and writing seemed an ideal way to make people's lives better and share those aspects of my own life that I found fulfilling: peace, tolerance, openness, equality, compassion, and the belief that all humans are basically good, loving, and deserving of a happy life.

With my master's degree in Social Change, I was determined to help transform society by working with low-literacy, low-income, adult learners so that they could improve their lives and the lives of their families and communities. In the early 1970s, I became one of the co-founders of the Community Learning Center (CLC) in Cambridge, Massachusetts and immersed myself in teaching, writing, training teachers, and counseling.

During my tenure at the CLC, I reached another turning point in my life. I observed changes affecting the students we served and experienced change in my own family. I was aging; my parents were nearing the end of their lives. Our student population was getting younger and dealing with more physical and mental health problems. To better serve our students, I decided to return to graduate school to study mind-body medicine and integrative holistic health studies. I

needed to act on my conviction that good physical, psychological, and spiritual health is fundamental to one's happiness. Without health and awareness, it is difficult to sustain motivation, learn, work hard, and reach goals. Our health not only affects our learning but also all our relationships with others. When we are depressed and angry, not only do we suffer, but the people in our lives suffer as well.

In 2003, I made a career shift and started a new position at Boston University's Center for Psychiatric Rehabilitation. My goal in changing my employment was to inspire hope in adults living with a psychiatric illness so that they would take actions that would ensure progress on their journeys of recovery. I would work to support this progress by sharing my own story of recovery, giving support, teaching new skills/information, and building a community using the classroom as a place of learning and affirmation.

Going to work at the Center for Psychiatric Rehabilitation was a real homecoming. During the first half of my life, I resisted getting close to mental illness because I had suffered so much during my childhood.

Without health and awareness, it is difficult to sustain motivation, learn, work hard, and reach goals.

But, by gaining new health-related knowledge and skills, opening my heart more to my aging mother, and reflecting upon my life experience, I realized I was most interested in the mind, its capacity to recover, grow, and heal. With this new understanding, I started to get closer to my mother, who during her last 5 years of life suffered from dementia. With the support of a Buddhist community and a loving husband, I began taking care of her and dedicating myself to my new students, who had the hope of recovery ahead of them. This is a poem I wrote about my mother a week before she died.

Betty and I

My mother...
I spent the first half of adult life
running away from her
afraid I'd be sucked in...
I spend the second half of my life
running toward her—
rescuing her from
a buckling knee, broken hip,
strokes frying her memory,
mellowing her to a marshmallow,
a sweet teary, diapered dementia
resident living only
in the present moment,
yesterday blank,
future lost,
unable to answer my whys.

Today I'm still left with
questions to explore
and motherly love

While my mother was in an assisted living facility and having occasional stays in rehabilitation hospitals, I began visiting her with my two dogs. I saw how the dogs lifted her spirits. The other residents with dementia and Alzheimer's disease enjoyed these visits as well. Some of the residents, who usually were silent and withdrawn, smiled and spoke.

Seeing the benefits of these animal-assisted visits, I began doing research into the human-animal bond. I decided that I would train my next dog to become a certified therapy dog. This idea came to fruition in January 2006 when my husband and I adopted a beautiful poodle from Poodle Rescue of New England.

A week after adopting Micah in January 2006, I enrolled her in dog training classes. By April, she passed all her exams and was certified as a "therapy dog." She inspired me to develop a new course, called "Kindred Spirits: Animals and Recovery," which I have taught at the Center for Psychiatric Rehabilitation for three semesters. She is a wellspring of unconditional love that I draw upon in my daily life. Micah goes to work with me once a week as my teaching assistant in various courses. The students say that by petting her soft, curly hair, they feel less anxious, less sad, and joyful. Her presence brings them back to the present moment where they don't think about their past nor worry about their future.

Friday afternoons, Micah and I volunteer on two psychiatric units at our local hospital. During our visits, she brings joy to the patients, helping them to relax and forget about their problems. Our visits give me an opportunity to talk about the Center for Psychiatric Rehabilitation's Recovery Education Program. I invite them to visit us to see an environment where hope is blossoming.

> It is up to each
> of us to discover
> our own path
> to recovery.

It is up to each of us to discover our own path to recovery. When we figure out how to make meaning out of our suffering, we can transform it and find our happiness. I think you will find that the answer lies in connecting to the love in your heart and sharing it with others.

CHAPTER 5
Building Personal Support

I took this
picture because
of the love and
gratitude I feel for
their friendship
and support.

photovoice

Barbara is a friend of thirty years and her husband, Gary, of about a dozen years. Both are kind and generous and don't keep accounts. I took this picture because of the love and gratitude I feel for their friendship and support in many ways. They cheerfully go out of their way to help me and their other friends.

—Diane, from *Wellness As I See It,* 2003

A Mother's Love

Valerie Fox

I think in everyone's life there is someone who has had overwhelming influence, either good or bad.

My mother was this person in my life. She wasn't a brilliant woman, but she was a woman who believed hard things could be accomplished, sometimes to the strong disbelief of others.

In my life, my mother tried to be understanding about my illness, but my mother wanted me to be able to live a life independently while dealing with schizophrenia. Her "tough love" when I was homeless was a very hard stance, but if I had had access to a home and had continued to live on the street when I chose in an acute state of schizophrenia, I am quite sure I would still be living on the street or dead.

My mother dealt with schizophrenia in an uncommon way, to some an unheard of way considered harsh; but my mother's influence, I think, was the strongest catalyst for my continuing to try to grasp independence and a full life while coping with serious, persistent mental illness.

The other quality my mother gave me when most other people didn't, was her trust in me—a person living with schizophrenia. I knew my mother believed in me. During the end of her life she sought me to be her caretaker while she must have known she was taking a chance since I could get sick. I did not fail my mother's trust.

While growing up, my mother was my best friend. None of my friends nor my brother understood why I loved to be with her. To me it was simple. She was very supportive, loyal, fun, fearless, and she enjoyed the arts and instilled in me a love of nature. My mother also instilled in me a fierce independence.

Then came the diagnosis, schizophrenia, which would change the course of my life. It was 1963, and I had been working at a good job in New York. In fact, I always had worked—sometimes two jobs to have the things I wanted. But when I became ill and returned home from the hospital, I felt so lethargic and unmotivated and so dependent on my mother. My mother allowed me to mope around the house for a few months, but then we talked.

"Valerie," she said, "you have an illness." "It's serious, but I believe you can live a full life." "How can I work or date?" I said. "I can hardly stay awake. Besides, when people know, they leave like my friends did." "Valerie, you will make other friends. Friends who won't leave," my mother said. "I want to believe you, but each of my friends left one by one," I said.

I knew my mother believed in me.

"Do you think that other people are without something they wish they didn't have to deal with?" she continued. "You have nothing to be ashamed of. You have an illness." My mother asked me why I did not look for a job. "I can't," I said. "I can't concentrate, I think, because of the medication," I said. "Suppose we call the doctor and see if we can have the medication reduced or taken in the evening?" she said. I didn't think I would feel any better, but I trusted my mother and said OK. My mother spoke with the doctor, who reduced my

This article was published in the *Psychiatric Rehabilitation Journal,* 2001, 24(4), 405–407, and is reprinted with permission.

meds and also allowed me to take most of them in the evening, so I was more awake during the day. This was my mother's first stance for my learning to be an independent person while living with schizophrenia.

My doctor told me that my mother probably had been the cause of my getting ill, but when I was with my mother I couldn't believe that to be true. But it was the '60s and that was the scientific thinking about the cause of schizophrenia.

With the medication reduced and taken during the evening, I started looking for work and did find a secretarial position. My mother had been right. I could work and earn a living.

Again I must state, this was during the early '60s when independence of a person suffering with serious, persistent mental illness was rare.

With my confidence in myself stronger, I started dating and met a man whom I became serious with. I told him about having had a nervous breakdown (term used in the '60s). To my surprise, he said my suffering a "nervous breakdown" did not matter to him because he wanted to marry me. I again spoke with my mother who asked me if I loved him. "Yes, I do," I replied. "Can you handle marriage? Caring for another?" she continued. "I think I can. I want to have children also." "Valerie, it's your decision," my mother said. I proceeded to plan for my wedding.

After two children and a number of years of marriage, I felt my marriage was an empty shell, and I decided to end it. If I stayed, I would never know anything but being my husband's sickly wife, whom people would tread very gently around—where my children would never know a happy, self-confident woman. Instead, they would know a mother who was considered "sickly and frail." I decided to take the risk of going on my own with my children. I had proven I could work and felt I had to be allowed to grow as a person, and I could not grow in my marriage. It was stifling. I proceeded to divorce, not telling my family what I was doing because I knew they wouldn't approve.

When I was legally separated, waiting for the divorce finalization, I told my family. My mother told me it would be very hard for me with two children.

While I hadn't confided to my mother my suffocating feeling in my marriage, she said she knew I was not happy. My brother stopped speaking to me, and my father was very saddened by the news, but he eventually relented and remained a stable influence in my life.

My mother remained in my life, but she left me mostly on my own. When I was feeling overwhelmed, my mother would appear for a visit. We would talk; and when she left, my spirit was renewed and my faith in myself was restored. My mother's praise always gave me an inner strength to fulfill my responsibilities and dreams. While I did not have much money, the chance I took was the right decision for me. I was happy, my children saw a happy, confident woman. I instilled in them the values that my mother had instilled in me. We did fun things together. We were happy. This continued for seven years.

> My mother's praise always gave me an inner strength to fulfill my responsibilities and dreams.

In many ways, even with dealing with mental illness, these were the happiest years of my life.

Then tragedy struck. In the apartment complex where I lived with the children, there was a stalker who would knock on my bedroom window in the middle of the night, one time cutting my bedroom screen. I was so terrified, I stopped taking my medicine against my doctor's advice so I would not sleep as soundly as with medication and could hear if someone entered my apartment. The stalker eventually was caught, but the damage was done. I already had started withdrawing from reality without knowing it. My ex-husband, while on a visit, took our children from me. I did not have the opportunity to say good-bye to my beloved daughters and they to me. I then descended deeply into a schizophrenic state and homelessness for a two-year period.

I think I went even deeper into schizophrenia than I would have if the children were not involved. I threw myself into the care of my personal God, the only person who could give me the strength to bear the loss of my children.

In the beginning of homelessness, my mother, who by this time was living in a senior housing complex, would allow me to stay with her most nights. She tried talking to me often about getting help, threatening not to allow me to stay with her unless I did. In my delusional state, I didn't think my mother really meant it.

One day my mother told me I could not stay with her anymore. That if I got treatment, she would help me. If I continued like I was, I was on my own. She told me this was a very hard decision for her to make, but one she thought she had to make for my sake. I stormed out of my mother's apartment, and did not return for the better part of two years. During my homelessness I never forgot my mother.

When I finally entered the hospital for treatment and was to be released, one of the first visits I made in the community was to my mother. She had my daughters there. I think if my mother had not made the "tough love" decision not allowing me to stay with her unless I went into treatment, I may have very easily died alone living on the street.

What I didn't know during my homelessness was that my mother went to court to gain visitation rights to see her grandchildren because my ex-husband refused to allow her to see them. My ex-husband fought against this vigorously, but my mother was granted liberal visitation rights. My mother told me when I got better that she was not going to let my children forget me. She knew I would get better, and she told the children that. Without my mother's tenacity, I doubt I would know my children today. Of all my mother gave me throughout her life, this was her greatest gift to me.

Once back in the community from the hospital, I lived in a housing program, which in time I wanted to leave, but was terrified of being alone, for fear I would become homeless again if I were alone. Again, my mother talked to me. "Valerie, why do you think you can't live alone? You always wanted to live alone. You were living alone with the girls for years before you became ill," she said. "I'm just afraid," I said. "If you live alone, possibly the girls will live with you again," she said. "I don't know about that. They had their little lives disrupted once already because of me," I said. "You were ill, Valerie," my mother countered. "Your children love you." Within a year I tried living in a single apartment. My apartment was nice, and I had a studio couch for my children should they visit. I visited with my children often, but they never lived with me again.

The first years of regaining my health after homelessness were very hard years for me. I was bringing closure to the tortures of having lived on the street homeless and ill. I had to learn that my relationship with my daughters was not going to be the same as it had been before the tragedy. It could be good, but it was going to be different. I cried many tears over my children, which my mother dried, assuring me again and again, that I did nothing wrong. I hung onto my mother's words until finally coming to a safe place deep inside myself.

While I was homeless, my mother had become ill with a heart condition, which I was not aware of until I regained my health. My mother, who had been afraid of nothing, became a frightened woman. I grasped this and knew I was going to be her support, her courage, and her strength for her remaining years as she had been mine. I remained my mother's closest companion until her death when I lost my best friend.

> The strongest legacy my mother left me was her belief that I could live a full life while living with schizophrenia.

The strongest legacy my mother left me was her belief that I could live a full life while living with schizophrenia. At times my mother used "tough love" with me when she thought it would help me to become an independent person while coping with schizophrenia. Without her counsel and, at times, "tough love" approach, I don't think I would have succeeded in my struggle for independence and the fulfilling life which I have achieved.

photovoice

It was a relief
to look up. I love
looking at the
world.

This is the first picture I took when I got my camera. I was looking at a squirrel nest in the crook of a tree, though the nest is hardly visible in the photo. But the camera gave me the occasion to look up, and looking up I realized how isolated I have become. I walk looking down, avoiding other people's eyes. I find myself counting steps or avoiding lines. Sometimes I talk to myself; sometimes people notice, and I feel ashamed. I forget to bathe, clean my hair, brush my teeth. I avoid old friends and colleagues because I'm embarrassed, and can't answer questions about what I'm doing now. Before I became ill, I was an avid observer: I studied plants, animals, film, art, architecture, literature, government, war. So it was a relief to look up. I love looking at the world.

—SQ, from *Picturing My Health,* 2005

Therapeutic Alliance

Valerie Fox

While a student in school this past year, I learned of something called a "therapeutic alliance." I would like to share with you what this alliance can do in a life, a life dealing with the sometimes overpowering symptoms of schizophrenia. As a young woman searching for my own identity, dealing with schizophrenia and medication side effects, it was difficult for me to fit into our family, and I am sure it was difficult for my family while I was learning to live with my illness. In fact, for about three years I would stabilize in the hospital, return to the community, stop taking my medication, and return again to the hospital until one day I gained insight that I had to take my medication or live in a revolving door to the hospital, community, and back to the hospital.

During these early years learning to live with the illness, I responded very well to the second psychiatrist I saw. I knew he believed in me that I could work, take care of a family, and live a good life. He made me feel good about myself. He downplayed the tragedy that had befallen me in the name of schizophrenia and instead only focused with me on the positives. I would struggle to work during the week, feeling the side effects of my medication while working, but I endured because of strong support and understanding. I had someone who seemed to understand how hard it was living with my illness. I don't want you to think he agreed with everything I thought or did. He didn't. As a psychiatrist is supposed to do, he allowed me to make decisions and sometimes not the best decisions; but he was there to listen, to discuss the avenue I had taken, and help me understand my actions. I did not know until recently that the relationship I had with this doctor would be known in the professional community as a therapeutic alliance. I only knew no matter what happened, whether I would have to be hospitalized, whether I got off my medication and suffered the consequences, he would be ready to work with me again in a non-judgmental way.

I remember in my journey with mental illness the most tragic time was when I became homeless and mentally ill because I stopped taking my medication for what I thought was a good reason. My doctor even called me when I had told him I was not taking it anymore, trying to reason with me. I already was descending into the depths of schizophrenia and did not have the insight to know I still could turn the illness around and stabilize.

During the course of a two-year period living on the streets, I called this doctor a few times. I can't remember the purpose of my calls. My mind has blanked on that. I do remember each time he would tell me I needed to go to a hospital to get better. Each time I would hang up the phone and continue my odyssey of homelessness and mental illness.

One day having clarity of thought, I sought treatment and was institutionalized. When I returned to the community in a healthy state, I remember I was too ashamed to call this doctor, knowing the stigma of having been mentally ill and homeless. I was afraid he too would not want anything to do with me. After months in the community, one day I called his office,

This article was published in the *Psychiatric Rehabilitation Journal,* 2002, 26(2), 203–204, and is reprinted with permission.

and his secretary who knew me put my call through to him. His manner was as it had always been, kind and non-judgmental. He asked when I was coming in. The heaviness in my heart from so much pain of living openly with the stigma of mental illness started to lift; and because of this therapeutic alliance, I felt hope for my future. The worst of my homeless tragedy was behind me. Back in this alliance, I gained confidence; I assertively sought my children and, in general, rebuilt my life. My doctor didn't care that I was the "homeless woman of Morristown." To him, I was a person who had been ill.

Over the years, thirty in all, I never felt he was just doing his job for money. I always felt he genuinely cared about me as a person, who was coping with a dreadful illness. One time I said to my doctor that I don't think I would have come as far as I have in my life if it had not been for his belief in me. He countered, "but you also would listen to what I had to say." A true alliance.

I remember one time prior to the screening law, unbeknownst to me, a family member of mine called my psychiatrist to tell him she thought I was "getting sick." That evening I answered the phone, and it was my doctor. Surprised, I waited for him to tell me why he was calling since I had not called him. He said, "Valerie, I want you to know so-and-so called saying you were getting sick, and I told her you were fine and to let you alone to live your life." I was shocked a family member had called him without consulting me, but I also had a most secure feeling that I was safe while in his care against the abuses of the mentally ill by well-meaning people. Again, his alliance with me enabled me to progress even further while living with schizophrenia.

On rare occasions, even on Sundays, I have been very upset about something going on in my life and would call him. He always has returned my calls and allayed my distress, putting it in perspective. I never have abused this privilege of calling him.

Today I still see this doctor many years after my first visit with him. So much has changed. I have become very stable, enjoying my life, willingly taking my medication, sharing my children's lives, writing

> He allowed me to make decisions and sometimes not the best decisions...he was there to listen, to discuss the avenue I had taken and help me understand my actions.

successfully, and working in the field of mental health. I rarely call him even during office hours; however, I continue to be monitored by him and still have a therapeutic alliance with him.

I have brought this alliance with me to my work as a direct-care counselor on a PACT (Program of Assertive Community Treatment) team. I also use it in my relationships in my personal life with my friends. I have seen persons light up, gain hope, make changes in their lives, and for some to know a few moments of peace because someone genuinely cares what happens to them, someone genuinely listens to what the person is saying, what the person is feeling. I have seen very difficult persons become very agreeable persons. Some of my friends and clients I work with have notorious reputations because of behavior problems, but I don't see that part of them. I believe it is because I view our relationship as an alliance and am not judgmental of the person. While I don't condone wrongdoing and verbalize same, I continue to show I like the person and to care what happens to the person.

In bringing closure to this article, I would like to say to other persons who live with schizophrenia, if you don't have a therapeutic relationship such as I described, perhaps you owe it to yourselves to look until you find a therapeutic alliance with your clinician, doctor, or therapist. I firmly believe without this alliance in my life I would not feel as good about myself as I do. A person does not have to be high functioning; a person has to like who he/she is and try to do his/her best. With a therapeutic alliance, what could be a chore becomes a partnership, a sharing of the burden of mental illness.

When I feel good
my journal comes
alive! It glows and
encourages me.

It accepts me unconditionally! When I feel good my journal comes alive! It glows and encourages me — allows me to write and write and write knowing there are many possibilities attainable for me. On hopeless, helpless days, it also listens — words, phrases — sense, no sense! It doesn't matter. Sometimes just listening is enough! The front of the journal is a Buddhist symbol — patron of the dead determined to deliver all creatures from the pains of difficult situations. All health care providers need to be aware of and refer to recovery programs that educate in holistic approaches.

—Ellen T, from *Picturing My Health,* 2005

Nowhere To Go Except Home

Barbara Markwood

"We are going to visit with him at Christmas," Kate mentioned early in September. Stabbing pain shot through my middle. Unrelenting tirades, nasty comments poured into my inner ear. Any sense of self drifted out of my chest leaving me weak, empty, more crazed each day.

Paranoia brought years of agonizing, silent suffering. I had no one to tell, nowhere to go. Without money or the courage to beg family members for assistance, helplessness fell to collapse to starvation. Voices ruled in darkness.

Coming around in cardiac intensive care revived constant deprecation. I had no one to tell, no comprehension. Central lines, nasal-gastric tube, little weight change, voices. Discharge maybe meant freedom. Leaving triggers did not mean leaving paranoid turmoil. A second more serious collapse, weighing in at 78 pounds meant 3 months hospitalization with, finally, an admission of hearing voices that were shouting at me to kill myself. My desperation tried three times in three hospitals to end this agony. Without ability to distinguish my self from my thoughts "clearly" to kill myself was the only way to kill horrible thoughts.

After three failed attempts, a realization of "no exit" was so overpowering, I was forced to cry out to God in helpless surrender (silently lest nurses might hear) into the darkness, "*I quit! Do your thing, have at it!*" (Years later, I understood this as a desperation prayer, which served, surprisingly, as a significant turning point leading to recovery.) Next, a psychiatrist asked me about voices. I put my head down, nodding affirmatively. A course of antipsychotic-antidepressant treatment hushed and eventually ended those commanding auditory and visual hallucinations with their intolerable anguish. Medications meant exit respite from profound inner battles. I could follow suggestions for visiting 12-step groups. Here I could tell my story, experience unconditional acceptance from others, and find support. Meetings gave me an opportunity to see how many others suffer, how important is the human need to give and take support. Specifically for me, I found a new vocabulary for expressing my feelings. I learned to even identify what it was that I was feeling, which introduced unknown hope.

> Meetings gave me an opportunity to see...how important is the human need to give and take support.

My credentials are personal experiences, offered to aid others. In hospital, a therapist recommended a pilot training program designed for users of psychiatric services to become providers as case manager aides in nearby Denver, Colorado. Assessed, accepted, and trained, I suddenly grew aware of a resurrection of possibility, a new life. After internship, The Region-

This article was published in the *Psychiatric Rehabilitation Journal*, 2005, 28(3), 303–304, and is reprinted with permission. It is based in part on Markwood, B. (2003), My mental health, *Mental Health Practice*, 7(1), 24.

al Assessment and Training Center offered a permanent position as resource coordinator. This meant coordinating state vocational rehabilitation, local community college and community mental health centers, brokering student supported education and job placement. It meant educational case management, leading a support meeting, individual counseling, developing positions in local community mental health centers, supervising internships, providing post-graduate counseling, and placements. Daily, courage grew in proportion to task success. Ten years later, I was hired (accepted) again, nearer home.

> I began to accept and forgive myself.

Employment educated me, developed professional opportunities for training in many states on recovery and dual role employment. Asked to train supervisor staff, I taught what I learned—identify discrimination, apply strengths-based approaches, WRAP,* and hope. Experiencing respect, trust, even feeling needed instead of needy, permitted directors in both agencies to apply my suggestions while teaching me professionalism. I began to accept and forgive myself. Furthermore, professionals became heroes. Some disclosed their own diagnoses, suffering, WRAP, and strengths. Some even hallucinated, some had hospitalized family members. At conferences, I learned that some state directors and executive directors had histories, disclosed, formed their own national organization. My own stereotypes were blown apart. I felt a new company

> Medication, education, skills training, hope, professional mentors, presenting, inner work, resources, and supports are doors to the feast of passionate wholeness.

of warriors. I can be a congruent professional among others who know desperation, share it, and are real.

Another mentor, Dr. Richard Warner (author of such books as *Recovery from Schizophrenia: Psychiatry and Political Economy*), provided a decade of successful care. He diagnosed, prescribed, listened, created, and catalyzed opportunities for a new role: collegial participation in writing, speaking, and employment opportunities.

Study, worship, daily journaling, singing, writing, serving on the Board of The International Step Foundation feeds spiritual hunger. Participation in several research studies through Boston University Center for Psychiatric Rehabilitation is intellectual food while reinforcing my sense of contribution. Russinova, Wewiorski, & Cash (2002) investigated the impact of spirituality on recovery. The mental health literature reflects that best practices may include spiritual components as personal supports and catalysts for recovery. Medication, education, skills training, hope, professional mentors, presenting, inner work, resources, and supports are doors to the feast of passionate wholeness, infusing meaning, value, and direction.

Reference

Russinova, Z., Wewiorski, N., & Cash, D. J. (2002). Use of alternative health care practices by persons with serious mental illness: Perceived benefits. *American Journal of Public Health, 92*(10), 1600–1603.

* Editor's note: WRAP refers to the Wellness Recovery Action Plan™ developed by Mary Ellen Copeland.

Embrace your
own spirituality as
a way to foster
self-love and
combat stigma.

photovoice

Although this picture is not of a church, I see God. I see God in the crafting of the stone. In the beauty of the lavender flowers. In the bloom of the tree. Somewhere I learned that God was in all things. When I was all alone as a child, I heard God calmly, repeatedly whisper in my ear "I will be with you always, loving you unconditionally." It was then that I knew that God was also inside of me. Now, as the horrible black hole called depression creates unbearable suffering, I try to, with God's strength, remember that I am worthy of being loved. For those who also struggle with mental illness, please embrace your own spirituality as a way to foster self-love and combat stigma.

—Catherine Imbasciati, from *Taking Off the Blinders,* 2005

CHAPTER 6

Setting Personal Goals

photovoice

Being off
medications…
priceless.

Multiply this by 11 and you get 11 bottles, 10 different meds, 18 pills a day (morning, noon, evening, and night) 126 pills a week, 504 pills a month. That is $156.00 in prescription copays a month, $476.01 a month prescription drug insurance, or 40% of my monthly income. Recovery being off medications…priceless.

—LMV, from *Picturing My Health*, 2005

Slip Sliding Away: A Journey from Professional to Consumer

Rachelle Weiss

There no longer seems to be anything fashionable about losing one's mind, and since I have never maintained the slightest pretense of being fashionable, it should be no great shock that it is happening to me. Nothing lyrically dramatic is going on. There is no bell jar lurking with a visible darkness. I am not even hearing voices telling me something or someone is after me, other than the messages I keep getting regarding an overdue Discover Card bill. Intellectually, I calmly (somewhat) recognize the physiological need to readjust the chemical imbalances going on in my brain with new medications. That same calm evaporates when I think of the effort that will have to go into making the darkness invisible once again (ok, maybe I am a little lyrical).

You may wonder why I believe I am losing my mind. My diagnosis is based on knowledge gained from my years as a professional mental health worker with a graduate degree from a reputable university. I also happen to be a professional mental health consumer with a diagnosis (all axes in proper order thank you) from a reputable psychiatrist (or 2 or 3 or 12). In other words, I know when I am rapid cycling.

Much of my career has been spent focusing on the "why's" of mental health. I have done a considerable amount of lecturing on mental illness and stigma. This often leads my audiences to believe I might have the answers to their deeply personal mental health questions. When they ask me how one gets and stays healthy, my response always includes the word *luck*. They think I am being smug. In reality, I am being as honest as I know how to be. I have been in the field long enough to know just what a critical role luck plays in one's health.

I have been very lucky for very long. My medication combination has been working for years. I was able to get a career, buy a house, and raise a well-adjusted, incontinent cocker spaniel. Everything seemed OK. I know, it may not have been the soundest course of treatment, but with the cooperation of a general practitioner, I simply maintained the status quo. If I noticed a slight resurgence of certain symptoms, I did what I had done most of my life—I wrote off my behavior to a (my) creative personality. Anyone who has played the psychotropic prescription game would do almost anything rather than go through another round of medication readjustment roulette (side effect consolation prizes optional).

Nonetheless, it became clear to me that slowly but surely the effectiveness of the meds was starting to lessen. In reality, I was cycling with increased frequency, and more and more of my energy was being spent on maintaining some sort of stability. I believe the appropriate cliché says something about my "luck running out."

However, even when I have been at my worst, I am still pretty competent in faking sanity (that temperamental, creative thing is useful). So now, even as I was decompensating, nothing dramatic or *big* was happening. Nothing large enough for anyone to say, "She's really lost it this time." My depressions are devastating, but private. My manic phases never get

This article was published in the *Psychiatric Rehabilitation Journal,* 2001, 25(1), 86–88, and is reprinted with permission.

terribly high. I spend money, I act and feel wired, I can't sit still, I have trouble focusing, and I annoy everyone—mostly myself. Have I not just described a lot of people you know? However, these people do not get to the point where they find themselves alone, unemployed, and almost completely dysfunctional. I have. More than once.

> I have a list of tip-off clues that say I'm headed the wrong way…

Now, I am not stupid. I did seek help when I first started noticing problems. I am a firm believer in symptom management. I believe it is a key to survival. I have a list of tip-off clues that say I'm headed the wrong way (insomnia, uncontrollable spending, etc.). Since I have insurance, I thought I actually would try to shop for a new doctor. I cannot begin to list all of the mental health practitioners I interviewed. (I was the one paying, ergo I was the consumer, ergo I was the employer, ergo I did the interviewing.) So much of it was a waste of my time. When you know with a frightening certainty you are becoming sicker, you do not like to find yourself wasting time. This is particularly important when you realize that should you run out of time, you can lose control over your own medical treatment.

When I went in to see the professionals, I was prepared with my history, my symptoms, my brain, and my education. I might as well have gone in empty handed. That my qualifications often were equal, if not superior to those doing intakes, was considered irrelevant. I was looking for respect and collaboration and help. What I actually got was one counselor telling me I needed to talk to myself the same way I spoke to my dog.

As I became increasingly desperate about finding good help, I culled the depths of my networking history to find a doctor with whom I could work and who would work with me. I hope and I believe I am in that phase now—working with someone who respects me.

In spite of that, I also know that I am in the middle of what can be the most insidious, dangerous, and painful part of living with mental illness. The "what happens next?" part. Simply put, I am scared. I am scared that I cannot trust…anything. I cannot trust my friends, my job, my abilities, or my future. I cannot trust my sanity. And here is the odd part: paranoia is not one of my symptoms. To clarify, when "crazy" is not black and white, and it almost never is, you cannot really see where your reality ends and another's begins. That's what begins to erode your trust in everything. In other words, if I think I'm a chicken, there's a pretty good chance I've crossed the line into *crazy*. However, if I am at work, and I feel my work is not up to par, is it:

a) simple happenstance, because I had an off day like everyone does occasionally,

b) truth, because the very nature of my symptoms are getting in the way of me doing a good job, or

c) an emotional overreaction/delusion—my work is fine, I am just getting increasingly insecure as I lose control over other parts of my life.

Take that notion and start expanding it exponentially through work, family, and friends, and you can see where the actual chemical imbalance in your brain becomes the least of your problems.

Professionally, I should be somewhat secure in my current position. Despite the support of my company, many of my colleagues and even the local mental health office—all of whom knew my history when I was hired, and most of whom are being kept apprised of how diligent I am about my treatment: I am still terrified. My colleagues only know me as the "professional" who says she has a history. They have never known me as someone who cries uncontrollably or who shakes from her medication. How will they treat

> I culled the depths of my networking history to find a doctor with whom I could work and who would work with me.

me if my "illness" or "craziness" becomes "in their face?"

My fear of their reaction is not any great mystery. Before being diagnosed I was fired 18 times. Before finding the right medications, I went through friends like water. What if it happens again? What if? What if? How long will it take to find the combination of medications that work? What will the side effects do to me? Will I be able to hold on to my job, my professional respect, my self-respect? Will I be starting over again? I am too old, too tired to start over. I have no reason to believe any of the above is going to happen—no reason except ancient history, and that alone has me paralyzed.

Typically, I do not share my fears with my colleagues. Only a few of them really get it. It is difficult to get past the us/them concept. They feel they compliment me when they tell me I've always seemed so normal. They see my visits into consumerland as some form of betrayal—can I be trusted again? They are in the field. They do not want the infection. Even worse is when they turn therapist on me.

But when I talk to my fellow consumer/mental health workers, we all get it. We all know that fear. It is not shame. It is not guilt. It is the simple gut-wrenching fear that anyone with any uncertain, potentially life-altering illness has when that illness recurs. But with mental illness it's different. When you lose your mind, you lose the essence of who and what you are. It is not a new theme. Sanity lost, regained, and lost again.

Yet, no one ever seems able to capture the day-to-day desperation and terror. Yet in the real world, some mental health professionals still find it difficult to understand why consumers become resigned, and why we might find it so unbearably difficult to keep on hanging in even one more day. Sometimes in the "real world" there are those who still hold the ill person responsible. Imagine depending on those professionals for treatment.

On a positive note and after much research, I have found a psychiatrist who treats me as a professional, who stays current with medication and is not a pushover. I do have friends and colleagues who understand and are supportive in every possible way. The difference that makes can be enormous. My doctor has tried a few different medication combinations. He listens to me and I do research, as do my friends.

I am still working full-time, my dog is well fed, I'm still trying the new meds. Also, I am still cycling, and I find certain things more difficult than I have in the past. I am scared. Very, very scared.

But I still get up in the morning and go to work. In a few days I will be conducting another one of the workshops on mental health and stigma for 250 mental health workers. Including this group, I will have spoken to almost 5,000 people in a 5-year period. I will teach them about the recovery model; I will talk to them about stigma and labels. I will talk about how it can happen to any of them at any time. I will talk to them about luck. Their luck, and how I hope it holds out, and mine and when it will return.

> I do have friends and colleagues who understand and are supportive in every possible way. The difference that makes can be enormous.

Taking care of
myself is a very
important part of
my recovery.

photovoice

Taking care of myself is a very important part of my recovery. The medications I have to take cause continual weight gain, and the weight has caused me to become diabetic. Being overweight and having diabetes made me get serious about how I ate. Moving into a group home where we took turns cooking with each other exposed me to different flavors and all kinds of ways to enjoy fruits and vegetables. Now when I want to get ideas for a dish I go to a local library and browse the cookbook aisle or call up my vegetarian friend for ideas for something good.

—Taira, from *Picturing My Health*, 2005

Recovery: Always a Work in Progress

Alex Morisey

I always am reluctant to talk about recovery in terms of mental illnesses because it can be very elusive. For me, recovery is a continuing process. There is always the possibility of relapse. Rachelle Weiss wrote about the element of luck in recovery in her article* (Weiss, 2001). There is definitely an element of luck in my experience and what I like to call "continuing recovery" is hard work. In my work in the Public Housing Tenant Movement, we always signed our letters, "Yours in the struggle." Recovery is a continuing struggle.

I serve as a patient advocate at Norristown State Hospital in Pennsylvania. I am employed by the Mental Health Association of Southeastern Pennsylvania. That job has given me some additional insight into my struggle with bipolar disorder. I was diagnosed with this disorder in my late 30s. I am now 62. I have been in and out of private psychiatric hospitals, and once in a state institution. My struggle with my bipolar disorder has resulted in my taking several different medications to try to stabilize my condition. Lithium and Zyprexa seem to be working at this time. I must have seen at least 30 different psychiatrists and more than 15 psychologists since I was first diagnosed.

It is ironic to me that the mental health system expects stability as a goal for recovery, but the system itself is by no means stable. My last episode of instability, approximately 5 years ago, occurred after my psychiatrist at the time recommended I stop taking one of my medications because I was doing so well.

That experience illustrated to me how much trial and error play a part in the search for appropriate medication. Psychiatrists seem reluctant to talk about the error aspect of the trial.

At this time, I seem to be at a good point on my road to recovery. Throughout my struggle I have had a wonderful, caring family and an understanding circle of friends in spite of the fact that at times in my illness I have hurt both family and friends. I also am blessed with a supportive spiritual community.

One big difference in my life now is that I am in a very supportive work environment. Probably all people diagnosed with a mental disorder have had unpleasant work experiences ranging from negative comments about mental illnesses to being fired or laid off (the process usually used to fire consumers). Work is such an integral part of daily life and can serve to help define a person.

> For me, recovery is a continuing process.

Being employed as a patient advocate at Norristown State Hospital is an important component of my continuing recovery for the following reasons: I am able to freely discuss my own mental health as well as discuss and learn about mental health issues.

- I am constantly reminded of the need to pay attention to my own mental health.

This article was published in the *Psychiatric Rehabilitation Journal*, 2003, 26(4), 427–428, and is reprinted with permission.

*Editor's note: The Rachelle Weiss article is republished on page 119 of this publication.

- The staff of the hospital, particularly the administrative staff as well as the Mental Heath Association staff, are very supportive and give positive feedback to me.

- A factor that is not often discussed, but is important, is that I get a lot of exercise, walking from the train to and from work, and walking a lot on the Norristown campus from building to building.

- My self-esteem is enhanced because I feel I am making a positive contribution to an issue that has at times had a very negative impact on me.

- The love and support that I receive from peers daily serve to provide me with tremendous encouragement for continuing in my own personal struggle and in my efforts to make a difference for others.

- After years of being in administrative positions in nonprofit organizations, it is a pleasure not to have to worry about budgets, personnel issues, raising money, boards of directors, and all the other headaches of being a boss.

- Finally, I am able to observe daily how medication can have a positive effect and the importance of continuing to take it.

There are many factors that are a part of recovering, including supportive family and friends, medication, therapy, spiritual support, as well as others. Work, to me, is of vital importance in recovery. Luck also may be a factor. I feel lucky to be at Norristown State Hospital. I prefer to say that I am blessed to be there. As in any aspect of our lives, certain individuals can make an important difference. I am grateful to Sarah Bourne of the Mental Health Association who hired me for the work at Norristown at a time when I was unemployed and at a very low point in my struggle. Sarah had confidence in me and encouraged me. She always provided positive support as long as she supervised me, and she continues to be a valued friend. Also Dr. Aidan Altenor, CEO of Norristown, has been a wonderful support to me. It is refreshing

and amazing to me that he takes time out of his busy schedule to give me positive feedback. He listens carefully to any matter I bring to his attention. He always makes me feel that I am a valuable part of the Norristown Hospital community.

I have worked hard at trying to achieve some stability in my struggle with bipolar disorder. This struggle is always a work in progress. It cannot be laid down, forgotten about, or viewed as complete, requiring no additional work. I am fortunate that I can point to some very positives elements in my continuing recovery. For me, recovery is a word that describes a daily or even hourly condition. Every day I give thanks for being blessed with a few more hours of stability.

> This struggle is always a work in progress. It cannot be laid down, forgotten about, or viewed as complete, requiring no additional work.

Reference

Weiss, R. (2001). Slip sliding away: A journey from professional to consumer. *Psychiatric Rehabilitation Journal,* 25(1), 86–88.

It reminds me how
lucky I am to have
found support and
medications that
work for me.

photovoice

This is my current apartment building in Brighton.
I value it because I was homeless for a period of about
three months at the height of my illness. It reminds
me how lucky I am to have found support and medications that work for me. So hopefully I won't wind
up homeless again. I hope that people could understand what's going on with the homeless and to try
and be more helpful.

—KM, from *Picturing My Health*, 2005

Coping with Mental Illness

Gwen Davis

"That schizophrenia!" my inpatient doctor exclaimed, "It's playing tricks on my friend, Gwen! This person your mind created, Shalom, is not real!"

The memory of this conversation slowly crept back into my consciousness as I sat on the floor, locked in the seclusion room in the psychiatric unit of Children's Hospital. I was covering my eyes so I wouldn't see Shalom's frightful glares, and I was screaming, so I wouldn't be forced to listen to Shalom's torturous inside information. All of a sudden, nothing made sense any more. What if, in fact, Shalom wasn't real? What if I were only imagining him? What if I really did have schizophrenia?

It all started when I was in 9th grade, when Shalom first appeared in my life. "You have been chosen," he had said to me, "You have been chosen to be part of my secretive, privileged organization. With my help, and with the inside information I will give you, you will be able to accomplish great things for yourself and for all of humanity."

With that declaration, Shalom began to relay his secret messages to me. At first the information was about how special I was, how I stood out from everyone around me, and how important the things I did were, but slowly these messages began taking a darker turn. Soon, Shalom began to tell me that my teachers and acquaintances were thinking terrible things about me, that they hated me, that the whole world was out to get me. From the feelings of unworthiness that I then experienced, I began to cut myself on my legs with a knife or scissors, with anything sharp that I could find, in order to make myself feel that I was good enough to be redeemed. And finally, I began to know that people whom I loved would die. "Your mom along with all your friends will be burned alive!" Shalom said. This last message, of how people would come to a painful demise, scared me so much that I began warning the potential victims. "Someone will have to die. Someone will have to die!" I whispered. It was at this point that it became apparent to the people around me that I was ill and that I needed to be hospitalized.

After the painful diagnosis of schizophrenia, after months of hospitalization, and after many lengthy medication trials, the psychotic reality that I had known, the reality of Shalom, slowly began to crumble. My doctors steadily had been telling me that Shalom was not a real person, but it wasn't until now that I began to wonder if this could be true.

> I felt shocked in knowing that my brain could be so dead wrong in its perceptions.

But I still was fastened in a struggle of confusion. It was difficult to accept my doctor's words that I had been hallucinating. I held onto all kinds of rationalizations of why my doctors had thought Shalom wasn't real. One, I told myself, was that Shalom was very clandestine in his activities, and only revealed himself to me. He thereby kept everyone else com-

This article was published in the *Psychiatric Rehabilitation Journal*, 2005, 28(3), 299–302, and is reprinted with permission.

pletely oblivious to his existence. Since I was the only one who was a part of his secretive organization, only I was special enough to know him. This, I tried to believe, was why everyone else thought I only was imagining Shalom, and why everyone thought I was suffering from an illness.

But as I was given medicine, a combination of Abilify and Risperdal, I began to get more and more muddled, for now I wouldn't see Shalom as much anymore. And when he was there, he was much quieter and no longer would tell me of terrible things that would happen to me or to others.

"This is odd," I thought to myself. "It's too much of a coincidence that when I started taking antipsychotic medication, Shalom started to go away. Maybe the medicine really is fixing my brain, enabling me to experience the world as everyone else experiences it."

I also began to realize that none of Shalom's threats ever came true. No one had died a terrible painful death, and I began to comprehend that there was no reason to believe that I was less worthy a human being than others. That's when I decided my doctors must be right—that Shalom wasn't real, that schizophrenia was playing tricks on my brain.

Coming to terms with the fact that I had a severe, chronic mental illness was unspeakably difficult in a number of different ways. Firstly, I felt shocked in knowing that my brain could be so dead wrong in its perceptions. For years Shalom had been in my life, and it had been crystal clear to me that he was just a regular, normal person. He looked like other people, he had a regular voice, and he seemed just as real as anyone else. How could my mind do this to me? How could it have gone so haywire as to have me imagine someone who didn't really exist? And it wasn't that he just looked and sounded normal, but we interacted with each other like two typical friends.

Secondly, it was hard to accept the reality that I was an ordinary person, not someone who was part of a secretive and omnipotent organization. All throughout high school, I had known that I was one of the greatest, most important people on earth; that I, because of my camaraderie with Shalom, was prac-

tically omniscient and exceptional. But now, all of a sudden, I realized that the way I thought of myself was not accurate. For if Shalom wasn't real, then I wasn't omniscient, I wasn't special—I was just me, Gwen, a regular person, who had regular abilities and possessed ordinary skills.

In addition to all this, it was painful to come to terms with how much Shalom had controlled my life. He had made me cut myself, he made me terrified for other people's safety, and he had prevented me from going to certain places, from talking about various things, and engaging in different activities. He had greatly circumscribed my life, I now realized, and he could have made me do almost anything.

At the same time, however, the understanding that I had an illness, meant that I had to say goodbye to Shalom. It was a very strange feeling that overcame me. On the one hand, Shalom had created absolute hell for me, yet on the other, he always provided me with attention and company—he was always there to tell me what to do, how to act, and what to say. Without him, even though I would not miss his terror, I would be alone—alone by myself.

> I knew that I had to start engaging in activities that again would give meaning to my life.

By all of this, I was disheartened. It disturbed me that Shalom wasn't real; it saddened me that I wasn't part of a major organization; it troubled me that Shalom made me do dangerous things; and it definitely depressed me that Shalom wasn't in my life anymore.

This new awareness, furthermore, radically shook the way I identified myself. If I wasn't a friend of an omnipotent person, then who was I? If I didn't have supernatural abilities to know what was going on in the world, then what was I? And if I was just a simple, mundane individual, which I invariably now knew I was, then what was my place in the world?

I knew that I had to start engaging in activities that again would give meaning to my life. I had to find new things that would help me gain a grip on who I was; other things that would fill the loneliness that consumed my heart; other things that would excite, stimulate and intrigue me. At first I was at a loss as to how to go about this—Shalom had been essentially my life for a long time, and it was he who provided all the purpose, friendship, and the excitement I needed.

> I found the art of writing. I discovered that anything from journal to memoir to poetry writing was extremely therapeutic.

Slowly, I was able to find daily tasks to fill me. First, I found the art of writing. I discovered that anything from journal to memoir to poetry writing was extremely therapeutic. I bought a pretty, hard-covered journal from Barnes and Noble and began recording my days. I would write about the ordinary things that I did from grocery shopping, to taking walks, to having a nice lunch. But then I'd also record my moods, the different emotions I felt, and also thoughts I had about what was happening in my life or in the world—how I felt about my twin sister getting into college, how I felt about the war on Iraq, and what I thought about different cultures. Memoir writing gave me a chance to reflect back over the past few years, as I began to record some of my past experiences—my trials in school, my hospital visits, and my struggles with getting well. And poetry writing was pure fun—coming up with groups of rhyming words, counting syllables, and playing with metaphor. Through writing, I was given the chance to take a break from the present, to express my creativity, to reflect on what had been happening in my life, and most of all, to validate my experiences and feelings.

I also discovered art and music to fill the gap within my soul. I learned how to crochet and was able to create colorful baby blankets and scarves. I also learned how to do origami. I'd buy scrapbook paper of beautiful hues, cut them into squares, and then delicately fold the squares into intricate cranes. Music was also a good distraction, and I would listen to anything from pop to classical to country. I'd allow myself to get lost in the beat, hidden within the melodies, and to become absorbed by the words. It created such peace for me.

Also, I realized that getting together with friends was a good tactic to alleviate some of the loneliness. I had had many friends from when I was in school, but had disconnected from them once I got sick and was hospitalized for so long. Now, I made an effort to get back together with them. On Saturdays, I'd invite them over to my house, and we'd talk about teenage girl stuff, play games, and take walks. Hanging out with them, though not as intense an experience as hanging out with Shalom, made me feel that I wasn't so alone and that there were people who were connected and dedicated to me.

Finally, having sessions with my psychiatrist was extremely helpful. We'd talk about my worries of being lonely, of my fears that certain things which happened in the past would occur again, and we also would converse about strategies, such as deep breathing and visualizations that could relieve some of the tension that I felt at difficult moments. Talking

> Getting together with friends was a good tactic to alleviate some of the loneliness.

with my doctor was very soothing; and in a comforting way, he let me know that no matter what happened to me, nothing was too bad, nothing was too horrible, and that we'd simply deal with whatever came up.

With all of the activities and support which now filled my life, I didn't feel as depressed, as disturbed, or as disheartened as I had before. I now had meaningful distractions and methods to make me feel more at ease with myself. But now that I had successfully pulled myself out from an internal crisis, I knew I needed bigger things: I needed to have goals for the future. I needed some larger ideas for what I wanted to accomplish with my life.

> I needed to have goals for the future. I needed some larger ideas for what I wanted to accomplish with my life.

First of all, I realized that I needed to finish high school. I had initially entered the hospital in the middle of my 10th grade year, and had been in and out of the hospital through what would have been my senior year, so I obviously missed quite a lot of school. Since I very much wanted a high school diploma, I looked into different ways I could possibly earn one. One program, which was recommended to me by a school counselor, was a home-schooling program offered by Brigham Young University. I took a psychology course through this program, but after I was through with it, I realized that I missed being in the classroom, being able to interact and engage with other students and teachers.

So, I looked at what the community colleges offered. I found that there existed a program, called Running Start, through which I could take college classes and earn both my high school and college credits at the same time. I then would end up not only with a high school diploma, but with an associate's degree as well. This sounded perfect. In the past, when I became really stressed, and especially stressed by academic work, Shalom would start reappearing and telling me to do harmful things to myself, so this time I made sure to start school slowly and only take one class at a time. I took English 101, and found that it wasn't too stressful, and that I really enjoyed it. This gave me confidence, for now I knew that even if it would take a few years, I'd eventually be successful at getting my high school diploma.

And that is where I am today—I'm at the community college taking classes. But as I reflect on it, I understand that earning a high school degree or even an associate's degree, for me, isn't a big enough goal—I want to eventually go on to a 4-year college and get the education I need to be a mental health counselor. From all of my experiences in dealing with my illness and being in hospitals, I want more than anything else to be able to help people like myself. I want to be able to reach out to others, who have schizophrenia or other mental diseases, and to be able to give back to them some of the help that I had received.

One last goal I now have is not only to help people like myself, but to try to help society understand mental illness better, and to come to appreciate what living with mental illness is like. I know that there is a tremendous amount of stigma, ambiguity, and fear which is associated with mental illness, and I want to help change this. I want everyone to see that mental illness does not turn humans into non-humans, who may be ignored or ridiculed, but that mental illness is just as much a part of life as anything else. I desire for the world to know that people suffering and recovering from mental disorders deserve being treated with respect and dignity, and even more, should be cared for with empathy and compassion.

Even today, I still struggle with the arduous issues related to my illness. But while I understand that I'll forevermore live with a serious mental disorder, I now have ways to cope and make myself feel better. By using my different forms of distraction, by keeping connected with my doctor and with friends, and by working towards my short-term as well as my long-term goals, my life is worth living each and every day.

I took this picture
because of my
admiration of
this brave and
determined
animal, who is a
role model for
self-determination.

photovoice

Gabriel is a resident of the Peace Abbey in Sherborn, MA. He escaped from a truck on the way to a slaughterhouse, refusing to accept the fate planned for him. I took this picture because of my admiration of this brave and determined animal, who is a role model for self-determination. Also, he represents the Peace Abbey, founded and directed by Lewis Randa, who uses the Peace Abbey in many ways to promote reverence for life in human and other forms.

—Diane, from *Wellness As I See It,* 2003

Being Bipolar and Dealing with Obesity: Personal Lessons

Melissa Anne Hensley

"Let's worry about that when you feel better." This was the answer that I got from my psychiatrist when I expressed to him my concern over the many pounds that I had gained after starting on an atypical antipsychotic medication. I have no doubt that this physician had my best interests at heart, and there probably were times when I was too unstable mentally to even begin to think about a weight loss regimen.

Yet it became clear after ten years of obesity and out-of-control cholesterol tests, not to mention low self-esteem and diminished energy, that until I got more physically fit, there was a limit to how much better I was going to feel. Between 1996 and 1997, I put on approximately a hundred pounds as a result of depression, a sedentary lifestyle, and a new drug regimen. The antipsychotic medication in particular made me ravenous; there was no end to my hunger. I eventually switched medicines, but I discovered that it is much easier to put on weight than it is to take it off. For years I struggled with my weight. I tried a medically-supervised liquid diet, which resulted in a manic, psychotic episode. I tried Weight Watchers and a low-carb diet, both of which had great results temporarily, but as soon as my psychiatric symptoms returned, my eating went out-of-control again, and I gained back almost all of the weight that I had lost. Every diet seemed to be a temporary fix, but I still used eating as a coping strategy for dealing with stress and anxiety. I lacked the skills that I needed to adopt a truly healthy lifestyle. Furthermore, I resisted exercise. I joined a gym for a while at the urging of my physician, but working out in front of other people made me anxious, so I quit.

In late 2006, I grew tired of my sedentary lifestyle. I was tired, too, of having to buy two seats to fly on an airplane; tired of being reminded of my many risk factors for metabolic syndrome; tired of having to wear shapeless clothes to cover my over-sized body; tired of feeling bad about myself. I threw myself on the mercy of the dietitian at the health service at Washington University, where I am enrolled in doctoral studies. I was barely out of a precontemplation phase (DiClemente, 2003)—I was thinking about getting more physically fit, but I did not really know how I would go about it. The dietitian was gentle. She asked me questions about my eating habits and about my goals. She unknowingly adopted a harm reduction approach to my weight situation. She did not suggest that I go on an all-out diet immediately. Instead, she asked me about the easiest place to start. One meal at a time, she and I established new guidelines for eating. We talked about basic tenets of good nutrition, and slow-

> I am convinced that eating more healthful food and getting regular exercise has improved my moods and boosted my quality of life.

This article was published in the *Psychiatric Rehabilitation Journal,* 2008, 31(3), 247–248, and is reprinted with permission.

ly introduced changes into my style of eating. At first, I could not stop my emotional eating, and there were times when I would eat a healthy meal according to my guidelines and still go out to a fast food drive-thru for a binge afterward. But around the first of the year in 2007, I entered an action phase: I made a commitment to myself that I would use the next year to get more physically fit and hopefully lose some weight. I have not always followed my personal guidelines perfectly, but more often than not, I follow them, and I feel better. Over a period of three or four months, very gradually, meeting about every three weeks, the dietitian and I re-made my eating habits.

> My therapist helped me to come up with a list of coping strategies that I can use instead of heading for the cookie jar or drive-thru.

I started exercising, too. At first I could only walk for about five minutes at a time before becoming out of breath, but now I am up to twenty-five minutes at a stretch. I joined my local community center, and though I still struggle to make myself work out in front of other people, my exercise routine is fairly consistent. I confronted my fear of being outdoors and started going for walks around my neighborhood, as well. I even signed up for the NAMI Walk in my community.

I also started talking in psychotherapy about the reasons why I eat. My therapist helped me to come up with a list of coping strategies that I can use instead of heading for the cookie jar or drive-thru. We talked about the shame I carry around due to my weight and former unhealthy habits. My therapist supported me through the months when I was trying to make changes, and she helped me to see that when I did have fluctuations in mood, there were ways to deal with that besides overeating. She helped me to incorporate a more healthful attitude toward food into my overall strategy for recovery. I still have to work at managing my bipolar disorder every day, but I have found that having more stable eating habits actually has made my psychiatric illness easier to deal with. I no longer have food as a coping skill, but then again, my moods are more stable because I am eating for nourishment. I do not have the ups and downs that accompanied binge eating.

Thus far, my story is not all that dramatic. From January to May of 2007, I lost twenty-six pounds. My total cholesterol, LDL, and triglycerides have decreased. I wear a smaller pants size. I have more energy, and I have become accustomed to eating less food, so I am not hungry all the time. I try to listen to my physical hunger as a cue to tell me when and how much to eat; this is a new habit for me, so I still slip up every now and then. I still meet with the dietitian every few weeks for moral support. She has taught me that losing weight and adopting a healthy lifestyle is something that you have to work at consistently, over time, in order to make it work.

> Change takes time…even becoming willing to make a change takes time…one should never give up on the possibility of recovery and personal growth.

I am pretty stable at this point in terms of psychiatric symptoms. I am hoping that things will stay that way, but thanks to my dietitian and my therapist, I feel that I have some new skills that I didn't have before that will help me in case I do start to feel bad. I am trying to make my new habits enough of a routine so that I won't have to sacrifice a healthy lifestyle to psychiatric symptoms, should they crop up again. When I start to feel lonely or depressed, I know I can make a cup of tea, spend time with my cat, or read a recovery-related book. I have started in group therapy for eating issues, as well, and the support of others who are dealing with similar problems has been very comforting. I don't know how much weight

I will lose or how long it will take, but I am convinced that eating more healthful food and getting regular exercise has improved my moods and boosted my quality of life. I am so thankful to my professional support people for being there for me when I needed help and for not giving up on me when my habits didn't change right away.

I hope that other people with psychiatric disabilities and their treating professionals can learn from my experience: that change takes time, that even becoming willing to make a change takes time, and that one should never give up on the possibility of recovery and personal growth.

Reference

DiClemente, C. C. (2003). *Addiction and change: How addictions develop and addicted people recover.* New York: Guilford Press.